True Tales™
from the
Polar
Regions

Henry Billings

Melissa Stone Billings

STECK-VAUGHN
ELEMENTARY · SECONDARY · ADULT · LIBRARY
A Harcourt Company

www.steck-vaughn.com

Acknowledgments

• •

Executive Editor: Stephanie Muller
Senior Editor: Kristy Schulz
Project Editor: Meredith Edgley O'Reilly
Associate Director of Design: Cynthia Ellis
Designer Manager: Alexandra Corona
Media Researcher: Claudette Landry
Electronic Production Artists: Dina Instinski, Linda Reed
Electronic Production Specialist: Alan Klemp

Cartography: MapQuest.com, Inc.
Illustration Credits: Pp. 25, 48(t), 56(b) Kathie Kelleher
Photo Credits: Cover (inset) The Granger Collection; Cover (snowshoes, compass, passport) ©PhotoDisc; Cover (background), p.1 CORBIS/Wolfgang Kaehler; p.3 ©PhotoDisc; p.6 CORBIS/ Roger Tidman; p.8 CORBIS; p.9 The Granger Collection; p.10 CORBIS/Museum of History & Industry; p.14 Culver Pictures; pp.16(both), 17, 18 Brown Brothers; p.22 ©Kim Westerkov/ Tony Stone Images; p.26 Courtesy Dartmouth Whaling Museum; p.30 The Granger Collection; p.32(t) Culver Pictures; p.32(b) The Granger Collection; pp.33, 34 CORBIS/Bettmann; p.38 CORBIS/Ann Hawthorne; p.40 Brown Brothers; p.41(t) CORBIS/Rick Price; p.41(b) The Granger Collection; p.42 Culver Pictures; p.46 ©Superstock; p.48(b) ©PhotoDisc; p.49 ©Kyodo News Service; p.50 CORBIS/Peter Johnson; p.54 ©Colin Monteath/Adventure Photo & Film; p.56(t) Popperfoto/Archive Photos; p.57 CORBIS/Christiana Carvalho, Frank Lane Picture Agency; p.58 From the American Geographical Society Collection, University of Wisconsin-Milwaukee Library; p.62 CORBIS/Darrell Gulin; p.64 AP/Wide World; p.65 CORBIS; p.66(t) AP/Wide World; p.66(b) CORBIS/Galen Rowell; p.70 CORBIS/Kit Kittle; p.72 Archive Photos; pp.73, 74 ©Gareth Wood; p.78 CORBIS/Dan Guravich; pp.80, 81, 82 Courtesy Helen Thayer; p.86 ©Kim Heacox/Tony Stone Images; p.88(t) CORBIS/Dean Conger; pp.88(b), 89 ©William Stevens/Gamma Liaison; p.90 CORBIS/John Noble; p.94 CORBIS/Wolfgang Kaehler; p.96 CORBIS/ W. Perry Conway; pp.97, 98(t) CORBIS/Wolfgang Kaehler; p.98(b) Archive Photos; p.108(t) ©Superstock; p.108(m) ©Norbert Rosing/Animals Animals; p.108(b) CORBIS/Stuart Westmorland; p.109(t) CORBIS/Galen Rowell; p.109(both m) ©PhotoDisc; p.109(b) ©Kim Westerskov/Tony Stone Images.

ISBN 0-7398-0855-9

2 3 4 5 6 7 8 9 10 WC 03 02 01 00

Contents

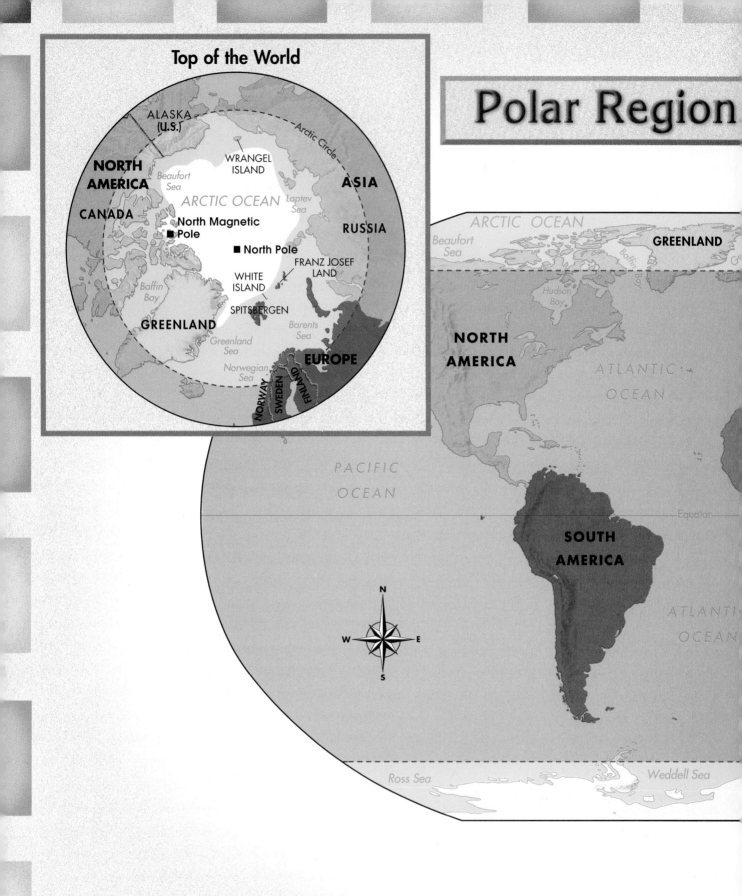

Top of the World

Polar Region

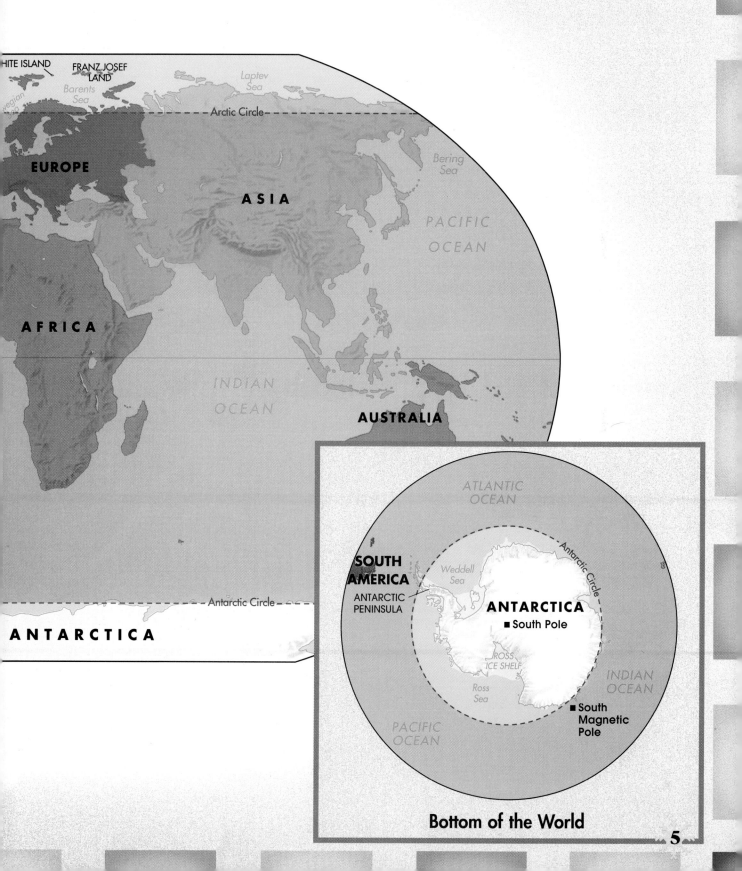

of the World

WHITE ISLAND

FRANZ JOSEF LAND

Laptev Sea

Barents Sea

Norwegian Sea

Arctic Circle

EUROPE

ASIA

Bering Sea

PACIFIC OCEAN

AFRICA

INDIAN OCEAN

AUSTRALIA

Antarctic Circle

ANTARCTICA

ATLANTIC OCEAN

SOUTH AMERICA

ANTARCTIC PENINSULA

Weddell Sea

Antarctic Circle

ANTARCTICA

■ South Pole

ROSS ICE SHELF

Ross Sea

INDIAN OCEAN

■ South Magnetic Pole

PACIFIC OCEAN

Bottom of the World

Trapped
by the Ice

The men on the *Polaris* were scared. Most of them had never seen such icy waters before. They wanted to turn back. But Captain Charles Hall wouldn't do that. He hoped to be the first person ever to reach the **North Pole**. So he kept sailing the ship up through Baffin **Bay**, past the coast of Greenland. Each day, there was more ice in the water. In early October of 1871, the men's worst fears came true. The *Polaris* became trapped by the ice.

A Long Wait

When ice closed in around the ship, there was nothing anyone could do. By then, the *Polaris* was far inside the **Arctic Circle**. In fact, it was farther north than any ship had ever been. No one would rescue the 25 crewmen and 8 passengers way up here. They would just have to wait until the ice broke up again. Luckily, the ship was loaded with cans of food and other supplies. They could live on the ship for a long time. But soon something terrible happened. Captain Hall became sick and died.

For months after Hall's death, the people on board the *Polaris* waited. There was nothing but snow and ice all around. The Arctic air was **bitterly** cold. The only noises were the crack of the ice and the roar of the wind.

Two men didn't seem to mind. Both were Inuit, **native** people from parts of the Arctic. One was a Canadian Inuk named Joe Ebierbing. The other was Hans Hendrick, an Inuk from Greenland. Neither man

The *Polaris* traveled toward the North Pole until it became trapped by ice.

was part of the crew. But both men had come along to help Captain Hall. They were used to life in the Arctic Circle. In fact, they had even brought their wives and children on the trip.

Ebierbing and Hendrick were not bothered by the long wait. But for the rest of the men, time passed slowly. The long, dark Arctic winter seemed to last forever. Even when summer came, the ice did not break up enough to let the ship pass. By October of 1872, the group had been trapped a full year. The crew had grown angry and mean. Fights had broken out. A few men seemed to be going crazy.

The Ice Breaks Up

Then, on the night of October 15, 1872, a terrible snowstorm hit. Some of the crew feared the *Polaris* was about to sink. They began to throw supplies off the ship. Ten crewmen jumped onto the ice to pull the supplies to a safe spot. Ebierbing, Hendrick, and their families also climbed off the ship to help.

Suddenly, the ice cracked. It split into many pieces. The *Polaris* was free! But seconds later, the **current** swept it away into the darkness. Twelve men, two women, and five children were still down on the edge of an ice **floe**. They called out loudly. But there was no way to bring the ship back.

When morning came, the group found that they were on an ice floe that was almost four miles around. They had some food that had been thrown off the ship. They also had two boats and two **kayaks**. None of this was enough to keep them alive, however, and the group knew it. The air was 50 **degrees** below zero. Soon, the cold would kill them.

Luckily, the Inuit knew what to do. Ebierbing and Hendrick gathered up loose snow. With the help of their wives and children, they built **igloos**. These snow houses kept the group from freezing to death. Ebierbing and Hendrick also knew how to hunt in the frozen Arctic. Every day they tramped off across the ice in search of seals or other food.

Even with the Inuit there to help them, the other men were scared. They were sure that they would never get back to the United States. They didn't listen when Ebierbing and Hendrick explained how to burn

Captain Hall stands with Joe Ebierbing and his wife, before Hall's death.

seal oil for heat and light. The men broke up one of the boats and burned it instead.

Another Long Winter

Soon, the Arctic winter set in again. It was dark all the time. Seals were hard to find, so the group often went hungry. When the Inuit did manage to kill a seal, everyone ate it raw.

Finally, spring came. The sky grew lighter. Birds and seals returned. Also, the ice began to break up. In time, the group's ice floe measured just 100 feet long. On March 30, they used the boat and kayaks to move to a larger piece of ice. When that got too small, they moved again, then again.

Meanwhile, the current carried them south. They floated down toward Labrador, Canada. On April 30, 1873, they saw ships in the distance. Hendrick jumped into a kayak. He paddled to a ship, which then sailed to the group. At last, they were rescued!

The next summer, the rest of the *Polaris*'s crew were found. They had made it to Greenland. Inuit there had helped them stay alive.

The *Polaris*'s journey to the North Pole had failed. But most of the crew didn't care. They were just happy to be going home, safe and sound.

Hendrick paddled for help in a kayak similar to this one.

Read and Remember — Check the Events

❄ **Place a check in front of the three sentences that tell what happened in the story.**

_____ **1.** The *Polaris* was headed for the North Pole.

_____ **2.** Nineteen people spent the winter on an ice floe.

_____ **3.** A *Polaris* crewmember fell into the icy water, but Ebierbing saved him.

_____ **4.** The *Polaris* was sold to an Inuit family.

_____ **5.** The rest of the crew reached Greenland.

_____ **6.** Hans Hendrick became captain of the *Polaris*.

Write About It

❄ **Imagine you were one of the *Polaris* crew or Inuit stuck on the ice floe. Write a short paragraph, describing your feelings as winter comes.**

_____

_____

_____

_____

_____

_____

_____

USE WHAT YOU KNOW

Focus on Vocabulary — Crossword Puzzle

Use the clues to complete the puzzle. Choose from the words in dark print.

bitterly	**kayaks**	**Arctic Circle**	**floe**
current	**igloos**	**North Pole**	**bay**
degrees	**native**		

Across

5. houses made of snow or ice

6. imaginary line around the area near the North Pole

7. units of measure for temperature or distance

9. area of water that is partly surrounded by land

10. originally living there

Down

1. painfully

2. large chunk of floating ice

3. point on Earth that is farthest north

4. water flowing in a certain direction

8. canoes with covered frames

Continents and Oceans

❄ The *Polaris* became trapped in Arctic waters near the **continent** of North America. Continents are large bodies of land. Earth also has large bodies of water called oceans. Look at the map of the world below. Write the answer to each question.

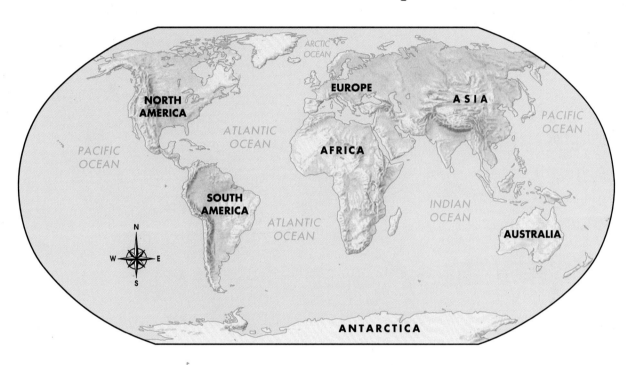

1. What are the names of the seven continents? _____

   _____

2. Which three continents are along the Arctic Ocean? _____

   _____

3. Which two oceans are along Australia? _____

4. Which ocean is between South America and Africa? _____

5. Which ocean is along Asia, Australia, Antarctica, and Africa? _____

   _____

6. Which continent is along the Pacific, Atlantic, and Indian oceans?

   _____

Arctic Flight

Salomon-Auguste Andrée had a dream. He wanted to cross the North Pole in a balloon. No one had ever done that. Andrée decided to start at Danes Island, an empty Arctic island near the northern coast of Norway. In 1897 Andrée took two men with him to the island. They were Nils Strindberg and Knut Fraenkel. On July 11, the three men climbed into a balloon named the *Eagle*. They were ready to risk their lives to float over the **unknown**.

A Fine Start

When Andrée planned his flight, airplanes had not been invented yet. So if anyone wanted to fly anywhere, it had to be in a balloon. But flying over the North Pole would be very dangerous. Many people warned Andrée not to try it. If something went wrong, the three men would be dropped onto the cold, Arctic ice. They might freeze to death. They might starve. They might be killed by polar bears or fall through the ice and drown.

Andrée knew all this. But he had been flying balloons for more than ten years. He believed that they could make it. Besides, they were prepared for a crash landing. The *Eagle* carried enough food for two months. It also carried tents, a boat, and **sledges**, which were sleds that could be pulled across ice.

Andrée's **expedition** started out well. The *Eagle* floated north across mile after mile of icy water. The men took notes about the birds and seals they saw. They also wrote messages for people back home.

Andrée sent some of the messages home by birds called **carrier pigeons**. These birds were trained to fly long distances. Other notes he put inside cork **buoys**. He hoped that the buoys would float south until someone found them.

In one message, written on July 11, Andrée stated, "We are now over ice which is broken in all directions. **Glorious** weather. Excellent spirits." In another message he wrote, "All well on board."

Problems Begin

The happy mood did not last long, however. Andrée soon found that the *Eagle* wasn't flying right. He couldn't steer it. The balloon just drifted with the breeze. For a while, the wind carried it north. But then the wind changed direction. The *Eagle* headed east. There was nothing Andrée could do to stop it.

Worse, ice began to form on the balloon. This extra weight caused the *Eagle* to lose **altitude**. It sank lower

Carrier pigeons

Andrée wanted to fly in a balloon over the North Pole.

On July 14, Andrée's balloon landed on the ice.

and lower in the sky. At times, the basket carrying the men bounced off the ice.

Andrée struggled to keep the *Eagle* going. But on July 14, he gave up. The balloon landed on the ice. By then, the men had been drifting for 65 hours. They were **exhausted**, yet the only way out of this frozen area was to start walking.

Bravely, Andrée and his men loaded up the sledges. They headed for Franz Josef Land. This was a group of islands over 200 miles to the east. No people lived in Franz Josef Land, but Andrée knew that a supply of food was stored there.

A Sad Ending

It was a miserable trip. The men were not dressed for Arctic travel. The temperature was far below zero. Snow and wind whipped at their faces and tore their thin clothing. Often, they broke through soft spots in the ice and landed in icy water. Yet step after step, they pushed, pulled, and dragged their sledges along.

As the days passed, the men became weak and sick. Andrée gave up hope of reaching Franz Josef Land. He and his men turned south. They climbed into the boat they had been carrying, hoping to sail to Spitsbergen, an island of Norway. But they couldn't find their way through the thick **pack ice** of the Arctic Ocean.

On October 5, they came to White Island, an empty, ice-covered bit of land. There the men pitched their tent and prepared to build a hut. They would have to spend the winter there.

But the Arctic weather proved to be too rough. Every day they lost strength. By mid-October, Strindberg and Fraenkel were dead. Andrée knew he would soon join them. He wrapped up his notes, hoping that someday someone would find them. Then he, too, waited for the end to come.

Thirty-three years later, sailors found the bodies of Andrée, Strindberg, and Fraenkel. Andrée's notes were still in good shape. So was some film Strindberg had taken. People were grateful to finally know what had happened to Andrée and his men. But they were sad that such a grand journey had ended in **tragedy**.

The men prepared to walk across the Arctic ice.

Read and Remember — Finish the Sentence

❄ **Circle the best ending for each sentence.**

1. The *Eagle* carried enough food for _____.

one week   two months   two years

2. Andrée brought along _____.

a radio   plenty of warm clothing   a boat

3. Andrée had to land the balloon because there was _____.

ice weighing it down   very thick fog   a hole in it

4. The three men made it to _____.

White Island   Franz Josef Land   the North Pole

5. The bodies of Andrée, Strindberg, and Fraenkel were _____.

never found   found by Inuit   found 33 years later

Think About It — Cause and Effect

❄ **A cause is something that makes something else happen. What happens is called the effect. Match each cause with an effect. Write the letter on the correct blank. The first one is done for you.**

Cause	Effect
1. Andrée wanted to send messages to people back home, so __c__	**a.** soon they became very weak and sick.
2. Andrée knew he might have to make a crash landing, so _____	**b.** he wrapped them up to protect them.
3. The men pushed their sledges for days in the cold, so _____	**c.** he brought carrier pigeons on the balloon.
4. Andrée hoped people would find his notes someday, so _____	**d.** he brought along extra food and supplies.

19

Focus on Vocabulary — Finish Up

Choose the correct word in dark print to complete each sentence.

tragedy	**glorious**	**carrier pigeons**	**unknown**
sledges	**altitude**	**expedition**	**exhausted**
buoys	**pack ice**		

1. Sleds used to carry loads across ice are called _____.

2. To be very tired is to be _____.

3. A long journey taken for a reason is an _____.

4. A very unhappy or terrible event is a _____.

5. Something that is wonderful and grand is _____.

6. Birds trained to carry messages are _____.

7. Large blocks of ice that are jammed together are called

   _____.

8. The _____ is something that people do not know about.

9. Floats used to mark something are _____.

10. Height above sea level is _____.

Map Keys

Maps use different symbols or colors. A **map key** tells what the symbols or colors mean. This map shows Salomon Andrée's balloon flight. Study the map and the map key. Write the answer to each question.

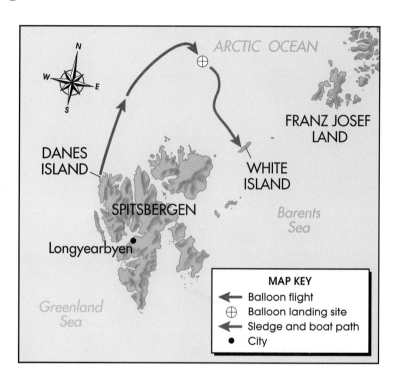

1. Draw the symbol for the site where the balloon landed. _____

2. What city is shown on the map? _____

3. Is the symbol for Andrée's camp sites shown in the map key?

   _____

4. From which small island did Andrée's balloon flight begin?

   _____

5. After the balloon landed, did Andrée reach Franz Josef Land?

   _____

6. Where did Andrée's sledge and boat path end? _____

The 3,000-Mile Walk

Crewman George Tilton was worried. In 1897 huge sheets of pack ice had formed in the Arctic Ocean, north of Alaska. The ice was beginning to crush Tilton's ship and two other ships. By September, the crews were forced to seek shelter on tiny Sea Horse Island. The 150 men were **stranded** there, thousands of miles from home. Tilton felt sure that it was just a matter of time until the men began to die.

A Wild Plan

Tilton went to the captains of the three ships. He pointed out that the group barely had enough food to get through the winter. In addition, most of the men had never been to the Arctic before. They knew nothing about living in this frozen land. "Captains, it is my opinion that half of our crews... will die before July 1 of next year," said Tilton. He also knew that no one from the outside world knew where they were. **Rescuers** might never find them.

Tilton then told the captains his idea. There were many large ships in San Francisco, California. Tilton would walk 3,000 miles to get help there. The captains knew the stranded group was in bad shape. So they agreed to let Tilton try this wild plan.

On October 31, Tilton set out. With him went two men from Siberia, an area of Russia. They took a sled that was loaded with food. It was pulled by eight sled dogs. Tilton attached a sail to the sled. That way, the wind could help push the heavy sled along.

The men became stranded when the ice crushed their ships.

Tilton and the Siberians headed south across the endless fields of ice. Some days they had good luck. They covered 25 miles or more. Other days, storms kept them from moving at all.

At one point, the three men had to cross an icy **mountain range**. It was too steep for the dogs to climb. The men had to unload the sled and pull it up with ropes. They had to pull the dogs up, too.

Going down the other side was even harder. Tilton pointed the sled's sail into the wind. That way it served as a brake. He was lucky the wind didn't change. If it had, the sled would have **plunged** to the rocks below, carrying the men with it.

A Storm Arrives

On November 14, a **blizzard** hit. It was so bad that the dogs refused to move. The men dug a snow cave to get out of the snow and wind. But by then, they had almost no food left. If they waited for the weather to clear, they would die.

Tilton knew what had to be done. He and his two **companions** left the dogs and sled in the snow cave. They hoped to come back for them soon. Then the men stepped out into the storm. They headed for Point Hope, Alaska, which was eighteen miles away. It wouldn't have a ship big enough or strong enough to rescue the men on Sea Horse Island. It wouldn't have any way to send a message back to California, either. But it would have food, supplies, and warm beds.

A Place to Rest

As the three men walked, the blizzard grew worse. "We couldn't see a thing," wrote Tilton later. He wanted to stick to the **shoreline**. That way, they wouldn't get lost. So every once in a while, Tilton stopped and dug a hole. If he hit dirt, he knew they were too far **inland**. If Tilton struck ice, he knew they had wandered too far out onto the frozen ocean. When he found sand, he knew they were still on the beach.

At times, the **fierce** wind almost blew the men right off their feet. They had to lie down on their stomachs and wait. When the wind slowed down a bit, they got up and began walking again.

It was so hard to see through the blowing snow that Tilton couldn't tell when they reached Point Hope.

As the three men walked, the blizzard became worse.

He bumped right into a house. To find the door, he had to feel his way along the side of the building. A dog began barking from inside the house. Then a man opened the door. He was amazed to see Tilton and his companions standing there in a blizzard. Quickly he let the men into the warm house. The two Siberians had bad **frostbite** on their feet and ears. One of Tilton's toes was frozen.

After two days' rest, Tilton and the two Siberians borrowed a sled and went back to the snow cave. They got the dogs and their own sled. By November 29, Tilton was ready to go on. His Siberian companions stayed behind. But two people from Point Hope went with him.

It took three more months for Tilton to make it into British Columbia, Canada. He traveled all the way to San Francisco, California. Whenever Tilton could, he sent messages about the stranded sailors to ship owners. At last, a ship was sent to rescue the men he'd left behind at Sea Horse Island. George Tilton was a hero.

George Tilton was a hero.

USE WHAT YOU KNOW

Read and Remember — Choose the Answer

Draw a circle around the correct answer.

1. What destroyed Tilton's ship?

a bad storm   lightning   ice

2. Where did the crews take shelter?

Siberia   British Columbia   Sea Horse Island

3. How did Tilton plan to get to California?

by walking   by sailing on a raft   by skiing

4. Why did Tilton dig holes during the blizzard?

to keep warm   to search for food   to find the beach

5. When Tilton went to Point Hope, where did he leave the dogs?

in a fishing village   in a snow cave   on a ship

6. What did Tilton bump into at Point Hope?

a ship   a house   an old friend

Write About It

Imagine you were the captain of Tilton's ship. You have agreed to let Tilton go in search of help. Write a short speech to explain to the crew what is going to happen.

_____

_____

_____

_____

_____

Focus on Vocabulary — Make a Word

Choose a word in dark print to complete each sentence. Write the letters of the word on the blanks. When you are finished, the letters in the circles will tell where George Tilton ended his journey.

frostbite	**stranded**	**companions**	**inland**
blizzard	**rescuers**	**mountain range**	**fierce**
shoreline	**plunged**		

1. The men might never be found by _____.

　Ο _ _ _ _ _ _ _

2. Tilton traveled with two _____.

　Ο _ _ _ _ _ _ _ _ _

3. Tilton followed the_____, or coast, to stay on track.

　Ο _ _ _ _ _ _ _ _

4. A bad _____, or snowstorm, hit in November.

　Ο _ _ _ _ _ _ _

5. The _____ wind was cold and strong.

　Ο _ _ _ _ _ _

6. The Siberians got bad _____ on their ears and feet.

　Ο _ _ _ _ _ _ _ _ _

7. The crewmen were _____ on an island.

　Ο _ _ _ _ _ _ _ _

8. The sled might have _____ to the rocks below.

　Ο _ _ _ _ _ _ _

9. The men had trouble crossing the steep _____.

　_ _ _ _ _ _ Ο _ _ _ _ _

10. Tilton stayed on the beach instead of moving _____.

　Ο _ _ _ _ _ _

Map Directions

The four main directions are **north**, **south**, **east**, and **west**. On maps they are shown on a **compass rose**. In-between directions are **northeast, southeast, southwest,** and **northwest**. The map below shows part of North America, where George Tilton walked to find help for the stranded sailors. Study the map. Circle the answer that best completes each sentence below.

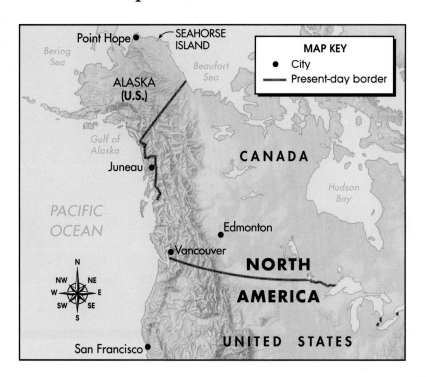

1. Juneau is _____ of San Francisco.

   west   north   south

2. Hudson Bay is _____ of the Pacific Ocean.

   south   west   east

3. Point Hope is _____ of Edmonton.

   southeast   northwest   southwest

4. To get from Vancouver to San Francisco, travel _____.

   northwest   southeast   southwest

To the North Pole!

Matthew Henson knew the Arctic was a dangerous place. Robert Peary knew it, too. The men had already made six trips together to the far north. Henson's eyes had been burned by the bright Arctic sun. Peary had lost eight toes to frostbite. A couple of times the two men had almost starved to death. Yet in 1908 Peary and Henson headed north one more time. With luck, they would become the first ones ever to make it to the North Pole.

The Journey Begins

As always, Robert Peary was the one who planned the expedition. Peary had money and power. He was a **commander** in the United States Navy. Henson, on the other hand, was a **former** clerk in a hat shop. Peary had hired Henson to help him on an earlier journey. In time, Henson became an expert at living and hunting on the Arctic ice. He learned to speak the language of the Inuit. By 1908 Henson was more like Peary's partner. "I couldn't get along without him," said Peary.

In the winter of 1908, Peary and Henson set up camp at the northern end of Ellesmere Island, Canada. This was the **northernmost** bit of land they could find. Beyond that, there was just the frozen Arctic Ocean leading all the way to the North Pole.

On February 28, 1909, the journey began. There were 24 men, 140 dogs, and 19 sledges. On the sledges were 10,000 pounds of food and supplies. The dogs would pull the sledges, and the men would walk.

Henson (center) and three men wait for the expedition to begin.

The temperature was 50 degrees below zero. To keep from freezing to death, the men dressed in warm furs from head to foot. They wore very dark sunglasses over their eyes. This cut down the glare of the sun off the snow.

Water and Ice

Matthew Henson

To get to the North Pole, the men had to cover 413 miles. They struggled to get their sledges over the rough ice. Then on March 4, they ran into a big **lead**. This was a place where the water was not frozen. Peary and Henson stared down at the open water. Neither they nor their sledges could get across. They would have to wait until the water froze.

A week passed before the lead finally froze over. During this time the group used up **valuable** food supplies. Peary and Henson were worried. If they found too many leads, they would never make it to the North Pole. They would run out of food and starve to death.

After crossing the big lead, the group ran into **pressure ridges**. These were places where huge ice floes had been pushed on top of each other. Some rose

50 feet in the air. The men used sharp **pickaxes** to chop their way along.

Other problems **plagued** the group, as well. Sledges broke down. Snowshoes wore out. Dogs became sick. As each problem came up, Peary turned to Matthew Henson to solve it. Henson knew how to fix sledges and make new snowshoes. He was also a master at caring for the dogs.

Racing North

As Peary and Henson continued, their group got smaller. That was part of the plan. Most of the men had come along just to carry food. So as the food was eaten up, those extra men turned back.

The remaining men struggled on through the cold, wind, and snow. Peary, with his missing toes, had trouble walking. He rode on a sledge most of the way. The others walked. All the men were growing weaker by the minute. Their food supplies were running low.

By April 2, only Peary, Henson, and four Inuit were left. By this time, the spring weather was getting warmer. Some days it was only 15 degrees below zero. More and more leads were forming. Soon there would

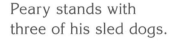

Peary stands with three of his sled dogs.

be too much open water for the men to make it back to their starting point. Meanwhile, the North Pole was still 132 miles away. If they were going to make it, they had to hurry.

For the next five days, they raced across the frozen water. Henson went ahead to make a trail. He later wrote that the ice was "rough and **jagged**." The men had to use their pickaxes to get their sledges through. Each night the men grabbed a few hours' sleep. Then they pressed on again.

A few miles from the North Pole, Henson reached a lead that was covered by thin ice. Thinking that the ice would hold him, Henson began to cross the lead. Suddenly, the ice broke. Henson struggled to get out of the freezing water. Then he felt someone pulling him back onto the ice. Ootah, one of the Inuit, had saved Henson's life.

At last, on April 6, 1909, Henson stopped. He was soon joined by Peary and the four Inuit. The six men stood on a sheet of ice at the 90°N **latitude**. After 18 years of trying, Matthew Henson and Robert Peary had finally reached the North Pole.

Henson and the four Inuit hold up flags at the North Pole.

Read and Remember — Check the Events

❉ **Place a check in front of the three sentences that tell what happened in the story.**

_____ **1.** Four Inuit men went with Peary and Henson on the last part of the trip.

_____ **2.** Ootah went ahead to make a trail across the ice.

_____ **3.** The men all dressed in warm furs.

_____ **4.** Henson fixed broken sledges and made new snowshoes.

_____ **5.** The group ran out of food.

_____ **6.** Peary walked the whole way to the North Pole.

Think About It — Find the Main Ideas

❉ **Underline the two most important ideas from the story.**

1. Henson and Peary spent years trying to reach the North Pole.

2. The men set up camp on Ellesmere Island.

3. The men were worried that more leads were forming.

4. The sledges were loaded with 10,000 pounds of food.

5. The trip to the North Pole was long and difficult.

6. Henson was an expert at living in the Arctic.

Focus on Vocabulary — Find the Meaning

Read each sentence. Circle the best meaning for the word or words in dark print.

1. Robert Peary was a **commander** in the Navy.

   leader   sailor   cook

2. Henson was a **former** clerk.

   excellent   poor   in the past

3. This was the **northernmost** bit of land they could find.

   flattest   farthest north   coldest

4. The men had to wait to cross a big **lead**.

   mountain   ditch   area of open water

5. The group used up **valuable** food supplies.

   important   very few   frozen

6. The men had trouble crossing **pressure ridges**.

   stacked ice floes   fast-moving water   powder-like snow

7. The group used **pickaxes** to help them cross rough ice.

   sharp tools   strong ropes   big sledges

8. Other problems **plagued** the group.

   troubled   saddened   broke up

9. The ice was **jagged**.

   smooth   sharp and rough   very thick

10. The men stood at 90°N **latitude**.

    distance from the equator   distance from land   snowfield

Latitude and Longitude

You can find places on globes and maps by using lines. Lines that run east to west are lines of **latitude**. Lines that run north to south are lines of **longitude**. All the lines are marked using **degrees**, or °. For example, Ellesmere Island is at about the 80°N latitude and the 80°W longitude. Study the map. Circle the answer that best completes each sentence below.

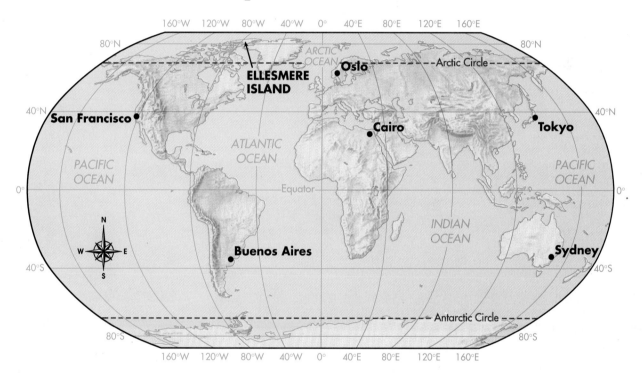

1. The latitude of Tokyo is _____.

  120°E   36°E   36°N

2. The longitude of San Francisco is _____.

  122°W   40°W   122°N

3. The city at the longitude 32°E is _____.

  Buenos Aires   Cairo   Tokyo

4. The city near the latitude of Buenos Aires is _____.

  Cairo   Oslo   Sydney

Almost There

To many people, the **South Pole** is just a point on a map. But to Ernest Shackleton, it meant everything. He very much wanted to reach the South Pole. Everyone who had ever tried to get there had failed. But Shackleton thought he could make it. On October 29, 1908, he left **Cape** Royds, Antarctica. From there, it was 747 miles to the South Pole. Each mile would put him closer to his goal. But it would also put him closer to death.

Many Dangers

Shackleton took three men with him. They were Eric Marshall, Jameson Adams, and Frank Wild. He also took four ponies. He planned to have the ponies pull sledges loaded with food and supplies. The men would walk beside them.

The sun was shining when the group set out. The sky was blue, and the cold wind was at their backs. "A glorious day for our start," wrote Shackleton.

Soon, though, the dangers of the trip became clear. Some days the sun was so bright it blinded the men. First, they would see double of everything. Then their eyes would water and feel as though they were full of sand. Soon Shackleton and his men couldn't see anything at all. It took hours for this **snow blindness** to wear off.

Other days, the wind kicked up terrible blizzards. Snow blew into the men's faces. It whipped across the backs of their necks. Their bodies **suffered** from bad frostbite.

Each day the men walked as fast and as far as they could. But it wasn't easy. In places, they sank deeply in loose snow. In other places, the snow was as hard and slippery as glass. Worst of all were the **crevasses**. These deep cracks in the ice were hard to see. If the men fell into one, they could drop hundreds of feet to their death.

The ponies also suffered. They were too heavy to walk on top of the crusty snow. With each step, they crashed through. They sank up to their stomachs in cold, wet snow. The wind and freezing temperatures took away their strength. One by one, the ponies grew weak and died. After they were gone, the men had to pull the sledges themselves. That added 500 pounds to each man's load.

Getting Closer

Shackleton stands at Cape Royds, the starting point for the journey.

The sledges held enough food for 91 days. That would be enough if the men could cover 16 miles a day. But they didn't come close to that. On good days

Shackleton and his men had to cross icy mountains and a high glacier.

they went 12 or 13 miles. On many days they were lucky to make six miles. To make the food last longer, Shackleton cut the **portions** they could eat each day. But that left the men hungry and weak.

For more than two months, Shackleton and his men plodded south. They worked their way across sharp pressure ridges. They crossed icy mountains. When they were about 400 miles from the South Pole, the men came to the Beardmore **Glacier**. This huge, slow-moving sheet of ice covered the area around the South Pole. For weeks the men struggled to climb onto the glacier. The **elevation** was more than 11,000 feet. The air was so thin that the men had trouble breathing. Each step became harder and harder.

A Race Against Death

At last, on January 9, 1909, the men stopped. They were 97 miles from the South Pole. With all his heart, Shackleton wanted to keep going. But he knew it would kill him and his men. Already they were in bad shape. They were exhausted. The sun had burned their skin.

Marshall, Adams, and Wild

The cold had frozen their faces and toes. They hadn't had a full meal in weeks. Their bodies were wasting away. To stretch their food supplies, they had been eating leftover pony food. But now even that was gone.

Sadly, Shackleton told his men to turn around. He knew that he had come farther south than anyone before him. In fact, he had beaten the old record by 360 miles. But he had not reached the South Pole. To him, that meant **failure**.

Shackleton didn't have much time to think about it, however. He and his men were in a race against death. It seemed clear that their starving bodies could not last much longer in the ice and cold. Somehow, though, the men forced themselves to keep going. For seven long weeks, they dragged themselves back toward Cape Royds. Sometimes they **collapsed**. But each time they managed to start walking again.

On March 1, 1909, they finally reached safety. They had been gone 123 days. Shackleton had not gone all the way to the South Pole. But at least he had brought his men back alive.

The men were disappointed that they had not reached the South Pole.

Read and Remember — Finish the Sentence

❋ **Circle the best ending for each sentence.**

1. Shackleton and his men traveled across Antarctica on _____.
   foot   dog sleds   skis

2. The worst danger was _____.
   crusty ice   deep snow   hidden crevasses

3. The men had trouble with _____.
   sand in their eyes   frostbite   rain

4. To stretch their food, the men had to eat _____.
   ice   bugs   pony food

5. Shackleton beat the old record of distance south by _____.
   360 miles   747 miles   500 miles

Write About It

❋ Imagine you were Ernest Shackleton. Write a letter home, explaining why you chose to turn around when you were just 97 miles from the South Pole.

Dear _____,

_____

_____

_____

_____

_____

_____

_____

USE WHAT YOU KNOW

Focus on Vocabulary — Finish the Paragraphs

Use the words in dark print to complete the paragraphs. Reread the paragraphs to be sure they make sense.

failure	**collapsed**	**snow blindness**	**Cape**
suffered	**elevation**	**South Pole**	**Glacier**
portions	**crevasses**		

On October 29, 1908, Shackleton and his men left (1)_____ Royds, Antarctica. They hoped to reach the (2)_____, the point on Earth that is farthest south. The men (3)_____ through terrible blizzards and frostbite during the journey. The sun caused (4)_____. The small (5)_____ of food left the men hungry. The group also faced the danger of deep (6)_____. When the men were 400 miles from their goal, they came to the Beardmore (7)_____. At the top of it, the (8)_____ was more than 11,000 feet. The thin air made it hard to breathe.

The difficult journey made the men weak and exhausted. Finally, Shackleton and his men decided to head back, even though they only had 97 miles to go. To Shackleton, though, turning back meant (9)_____. Still, the return trip was a struggle. The men (10)_____ on the ice many times on the way. They barely made it back alive.

Antarctic Circle

❄ Antarctica is a very cold continent in the most southern part of Earth. The **Antarctic Circle** is an imaginary line that surrounds Antarctica. The line is drawn near the 66°S latitude. In the center of the Antarctic Circle is the South Pole. Study the map below. Circle the answer to each question.

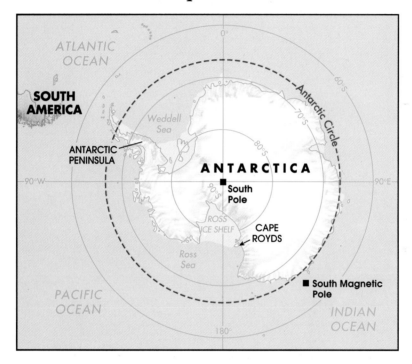

1. Which continent is very near Antarctica?

   Africa   Asia   South America

2. The longitudes 0°, 90°W, 180°, and 90°E all meet at a single point. What is this point called?

   South Pole   South Magnetic Pole   Ross Ice Shelf

3. Which area is completely within the Antarctic Circle?

   South America   Ross Ice Shelf   Antarctic Peninsula

4. Based on the map, at which latitude is the South Pole?

   60°S   70°S   90°S

Japan Enters the Race

Japanese explorer Nobu Shirase didn't have much to work with. His boat was very small. He had almost no money. He didn't have good equipment. But Shirase didn't care. He was determined to explore Antarctica. On December 1, 1910, he set out from Tokyo, Japan. As he left Tokyo Bay, Shirase knew that he and his men might not make it back alive. But he and the crew were eager to begin their adventure on the cold and icy **continent**.

A Lonely Goodbye

Shirase was an officer in the Japanese army. He had never been south of the **Antarctic Circle**. But men from many other countries had gone there. England, Sweden, and France had sent explorers to Antarctica. So had Germany, Russia, and the United States. Many of these explorers had tried to go all the way to the South Pole. No one had made it yet. Shirase hoped to be the first.

The people of Japan did not support Shirase's plans. They had no interest in exploring faraway lands. When Shirase headed out, only a few students showed up to cheer. He called it "the saddest and most **dismal** sort of a send-off" any polar explorer ever had.

With Shirase went 26 crewmen. They took off in an old sailing boat. Shirase named it *Kainan Maru*, which means "Southern Pioneer." The boat was just 100 feet long. It wasn't built to stand rough storms and icy seas.

Bad weather plagued the men from the start. They sailed through storm after storm. Cold wind and high

Shirase's vessel, the *Kainan Maru*, was an old sailing boat.

waves rocked the small boat. At times it looked like the **vessel** might tip over. Then, on February 26, 1911, the men saw their first **iceberg**. This big chunk of floating ice presented a new danger. If an iceberg hit the *Kainan Maru*, it could smash the ship to pieces.

Soon the water was dotted with icebergs. Some were huge. One rose 250 feet out of the water. Captain Nomura was in charge of steering the ship. Somehow, he managed to stay clear of all the icebergs. On March 6, he brought the *Kainan Maru* within sight of Antarctica's Cape Adare.

To Australia

The waters around Cape Adare were very rough. It was too dangerous to land. So the *Kainan Maru* sailed on. Shirase hoped to make it to McMurdo **Sound**. This long, wide stretch of water was further down the coast. There, Shirase hoped to land. Then he would march out across the ice-covered continent toward the South Pole.

But the farther south the men went, the worse the weather became. Snow fell without end. Icy wind

An iceberg

rattled the ship. More and more icebergs filled the water. There was no way the *Kainan Maru* could keep going. So Shirase ordered Nomura to sail to Australia. The men could rest there a while and wait for money from Japan. Then they would try again to reach Antarctica.

Becoming a Hero

The people of Australia did not welcome Shirase. In fact, they made fun of his plans. No one believed that Shirase and his men were good explorers. No one thought that they belonged in the **barren** world of Antarctica.

Even Shirase must have wondered if the whole trip was a waste of time. While he waited in Australia, two other men were headed for the South Pole. One of them would surely succeed. Indeed, on December 14, 1911, Norway's Roald Amundsen would become the first person to reach the South Pole.

Sadly, Shirase gave up the idea of being the first person to reach the South Pole. Still, he was determined

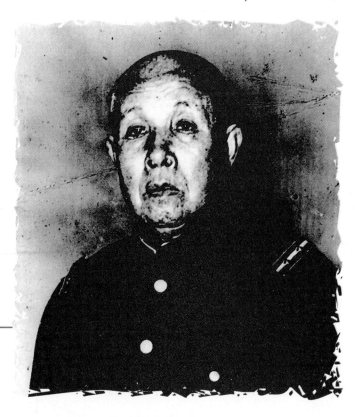

Nobu Shirase was determined to explore the continent.

to explore the continent. He decided to do **scientific** work there instead. He would take pictures and gather as much information as he could. So in November of 1911, Shirase returned to Antarctica.

This time the *Kainan Maru* made it past McMurdo Sound. The ship sailed to the Ross **Ice Shelf**. This huge wall of ice is many miles long. It was 300 feet high where the ship stopped. Other explorers believed that it was impossible to climb this steep part of the wall. Shirase wanted prove he could do it. He and his men struggled to cut a **zigzag** path up the wall. It took them sixty long hours. But at last, they made it to the top.

Once on the ice shelf, Shirase was hit by terrible blizzards. Still, he traveled 160 miles inland before turning north again. On February 2, 1912, he and his men finally sailed for home. They brought back a lot of information about the Antarctic continent. Most importantly, Shirase and his men had proven that they were good explorers. When Shirase returned to Tokyo Bay, he was greeted as a hero.

Shirase decided to climb the Ross Ice Shelf, a huge wall of ice.

Read and Remember — Choose the Answer

Draw a circle around the correct answer.

1. Who supported Nobu Shirase's plan to explore Antarctica?

   all of Japan   Australians   a few students

2. In what kind of ship did Shirase travel?

   an oil tanker   an old sailing boat   a large cruise ship

3. What did Shirase worry would destroy his ship?

   icebergs   large whales   pressure ridges

4. Who became the first person to reach the South Pole?

   Nobu Shirase   Roald Amundsen   Captain Nomura

5. What did Shirase do in Antarctica?

   climbed the Ross Ice Shelf   studied icebergs   found fossils

6. How was Shirase greeted when he returned to Japan?

   as a stranger   as a failure   as a hero

Think About It — Find the Sequence

Number the sentences to show the correct order from the story. The first one is done for you.

_____ The men cut a zigzag path up the Ross Ice Shelf.

__1__ Nobu Shirase left Tokyo in the *Kainan Maru.*

_____ Shirase returned to do scientific work in Antarctica.

_____ The crew of the *Kainan Maru* saw their first iceberg.

_____ Shirase traveled 160 miles inland in Antarctica.

_____ The men headed to Australia after sailing through weeks of bad weather.

Focus on Vocabulary — Match Up

Match each word with its meaning. Write the correct letter on the blank.

_____ **1.** sound

_____ **2.** dismal

_____ **3.** zigzag

_____ **4.** barren

_____ **5.** scientific

_____ **6.** vessel

_____ **7.** iceberg

_____ **8.** continent

_____ **9.** Antarctic Circle

_____ **10.** ice shelf

a. ship

b. very large body of land

c. causing gloom

d. huge block of floating ice

e. imaginary line around the area near the South Pole

f. long, wide stretch of water that connects larger bodies of water

g. huge wall of ice

h. moving with sharp turns

i. not able to grow anything

j. having to do with science

USE A MAP

Hemispheres

Earth can be divided into **hemispheres**. The area north of the **equator** is the Northern Hemisphere. The area south of the equator is the Southern Hemisphere. Earth can also be divided into the Eastern Hemisphere and the Western Hemisphere. Study the map below. Write the answer to each question.

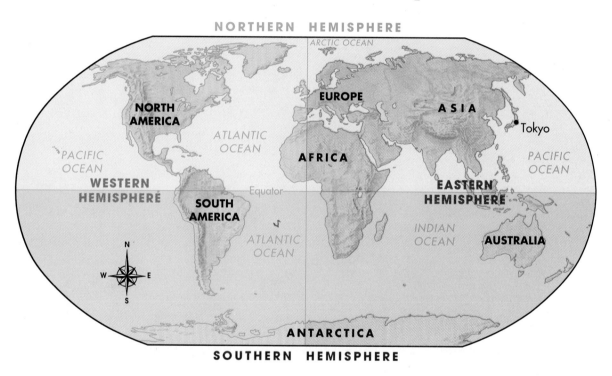

1. Is the Arctic Ocean in the Northern or Southern Hemisphere? _____

_____

2. Is most of Africa in the Western or Eastern Hemisphere? _____

_____

3. Find Tokyo on the map. Is Tokyo in the Northern or Southern

Hemisphere? _____

4. In which two hemispheres is Australia? _____

5. In which three hemispheres is Antarctica? _____

_____

53

In Search of Her Hero

In 1924 Louise Arner Boyd fell in love with the Arctic. It happened when she went on a **cruise** to Greenland, Iceland, and Lapland. As the ship cut through the icy waters, Boyd glanced all around. It was her first look at the sparkling white world of pack ice and polar bears. From then on, the Arctic was her favorite place to visit. But as Boyd learned, it was a place where death can come to even the most experienced traveler.

Bad News

After her 1924 trip, Boyd went back to the Arctic several times. She didn't go just for fun, though. She went as an explorer. Boyd took cameras and film with her. She photographed huge glaciers and icy **cliffs**. She took pictures of Arctic plant and animal life. Her photos gave important information about Arctic land and sea.

In June of 1928, Boyd was in the country of Norway in Europe. She was about to leave on one of her polar expeditions. But suddenly, she heard terrible news. Norway's Roald Amundsen was lost somewhere in the cold, **hostile** Arctic.

Boyd couldn't believe it. Amundsen was one of the most famous explorers in the world. In 1911 he had become the first person to reach the South Pole. He had also spent years exploring the Arctic. In 1926 he even flew over the North Pole in a small, light **airship**. Boyd had never met Amundsen. But he was one of her heroes.

Sadly, Boyd listened to the story of Amundsen's **disappearance**. He and five other men had taken off in a plane on June 18, 1928. They were trying to help an Italian explorer named Umberto Nobile, whose airship had crashed in the far north in May. Amundsen was rushing to the rescue. But something had gone wrong. Now Amundsen and his group were missing, too.

Boyd did not **hesitate**. Right away she offered to help look for her hero. She put aside plans for her own expedition. She told Norway's leaders that she would search wherever they needed her.

On July 1, Boyd sailed from Norway. She went to Spitsbergen, a group of islands far north of Norway. There, three Norwegian officers joined her crew. Then Boyd turned west toward the Greenland Sea.

Roald Amundsen

Staring Across the Sea

The waters of the Greenland Sea were cold and unfriendly. Huge blocks of ice groaned as they floated in the waves. The wind was bitterly cold as it whistled

Boyd offered to help search for Amundsen in the Arctic.

One area Boyd searched was Franz Josef Land.

across the water. From time to time, Boyd saw search planes passing overhead. She also saw other ships that were taking part in the search. But she found no sign of Roald Amundsen or the five other men.

Boyd did not want to give up. After exploring the Greenland Sea, she turned her ship toward the northeast. She headed up toward Franz Josef Land. This barren set of islands was hundreds of miles away.

Day after day, Boyd and her crew looked out over the thick, hard ice. They searched for some trace of Amundsen and his group. "Four of us stood watch around the clock," she wrote. "We would just stand there and look."

Boyd's eyes began to play tricks on her. The Arctic light made everything look strange. She thought she saw all kinds of things that weren't really there. "Ice does such **eerie** things," she said.

Sometimes she thought she saw tents in the distance. Each time, her hopes would rise. Quickly, she would send members of her crew off in small boats to see what was there. "But it always turned out the same," Boyd wrote. "Strange **formations** of the ice, nothing more." Amundsen was nowhere to be found.

A Hard Lesson

Boyd searched for Amundsen for almost three months. On September 22, Louise Arner Boyd finally returned to Norway. She had looked everywhere she could to find her hero. She had covered 10,000 miles. By the time Boyd reached Norway, Umberto Nobile had been rescued. But Amundsen and his group were never found.

Boyd's journey had helped her understand the beauty of the icy Arctic Ocean. She had learned how to **navigate** deep in the Arctic waters. She had even lived through a fire that sprang up on board her ship. All these lessons would help her on future expeditions. But Boyd had learned one other lesson, as well. No one, not even the great Roald Amundsen, was safe in the **harsh** Arctic world.

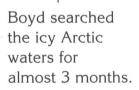

Boyd searched the icy Arctic waters for almost 3 months.

Read and Remember — Check the Events

❄ **Place a check in front of the three sentences that tell what happened in the story.**

_____ **1.** Louise Arner Boyd took photographs in the Arctic.

_____ **2.** Umberto Nobile was never found.

_____ **3.** Boyd helped search for Roald Amundsen.

_____ **4.** People in Norway were sad when Boyd disappeared.

_____ **5.** Boyd traveled across ice and snow to reach the South Pole.

_____ **6.** Boyd found that her eyes played tricks on her in the strange Arctic light.

Write About It

❄ **Imagine you were a reporter in the 1920s. You are about to interview Louise Arner Boyd. Write three questions you would most like to ask her.**

1. _____

_____

2. _____

_____

3. _____

_____

Focus on Vocabulary — Finish Up

Choose the correct word in dark print to complete each sentence.

eerie	**hostile**	**disappearance**	**navigate**
harsh	**cruise**	**formations**	**hesitate**
cliffs	**airship**		

1. An _____ is a large flying machine.

2. A _____ is a slow trip on a boat or ship for fun.

3. To guide a ship is to _____.

4. To stop and wait before acting is to _____.

5. Something that is very unfriendly is _____.

6. Steep walls of ice or rock are called _____.

7. Something that is strange in a scary way is _____.

8. If something is rough and not pleasant, it is _____.

9. The act of going out of sight is a _____.

10. Things that have been shaped are _____.

Arctic Circle

The cold, icy Arctic area is the most northern part of Earth. The **Arctic Circle** is an imaginary line that surrounds the Arctic area. The line is drawn near the latitude 66°N. In the center of the Arctic Circle is the North Pole. Study the map below. Circle the answer to each question.

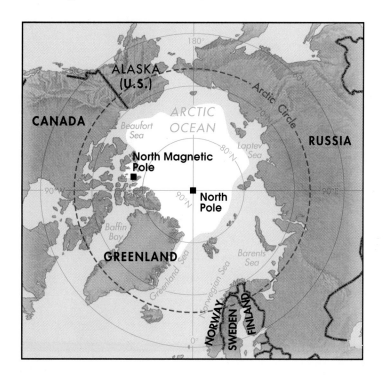

1. Which country is partly within the Arctic Circle?

   Mexico   Japan   Russia

2. The longitudes 0°, 90°W, 180°, and 90°E all meet at a single point. What is this point called?

   Greenland   North Pole   North Magnetic Pole

3. Which sea is near Norway?

   Norwegian Sea   Laptev Sea   Beaufort Sea

4. Based on the map, at which latitude is the North Pole?

   60°N   70°N   90°N

Trouble in Arctic Waters

On August 25, 1949, a bad storm rocked the Arctic waters near Norway. High waves crashed, and cold winds blew. Below the rough surface, the United States **submarine** *Cochino* struggled to stay on **course**. Rafael Benitez was in charge of the U.S.S. *Cochino*. He was testing how the submarine handled Arctic waters. But at 8:01 A.M., Benitez felt the submarine shake. Suddenly, he and his men were fighting for their lives.

Trouble Begins

The shaking that Rafael Benitez felt came from an **explosion** on board the U.S.S. *Cochino*. For some reason, dangerous gas had begun to leak into one of the **battery** rooms. The gas had exploded. The explosion had caused a fire. Black smoke, gas, and waves of heat now spilled out of the battery room.

Benitez knew he and his men were in trouble. The *Cochino* was 400 miles north of the Arctic Circle. The nearest land, Norway, was 200 miles away. Only one other submarine, the U.S.S. *Tusk*, was nearby. Benitez sent an emergency message to the *Tusk*, asking for help. But he couldn't tell if the message got through.

Benitez ordered the crew to bring the *Cochino* to the surface of the water. The storm's **gales** rocked the submarine wildly. But at least the men could get fresh air. He then ordered his crew to come up onto the main deck, away from the dangerous gas.

Eighteen men stayed below. They tried to bring the fire under control. The sixty other men began

The crew stands proudly as the *Cochino* first sets sail.

to gather on the deck. Some men had passed out from breathing too much gas. They were carried up by their fellow crewmen.

Benitez looked at the men as they came out onto the deck. They were shivering in the freezing temperatures. Many had been asleep. They hadn't had time to dress. So they were wearing nothing but underwear. They struggled to stay on their feet as high waves rocked the submarine back and forth. Icy water splashed up onto the deck, covering their feet.

Benitez knew a strong wave could wash these men **overboard** at any moment. Thinking quickly, he ordered an officer to get some rope. Then he had the officer tie the men to the railing.

Meanwhile, the *Tusk* had come up to the surface of the water. It tried to head over to the *Cochino*. But the storm made the *Tusk* bob and roll again and again. Then a huge wave knocked some crewmen into the icy water. Only six men could be rescued. Seven others died.

Fighting Cold, Fighting Fire

For five hours, Benitez kept his men **lashed** to the railing. Rain poured down on them. Cold waves splashed over them. Wind whipped across their faces. By 1:50 P.M., Benitez knew he had to do something. The men couldn't last much longer out in the storm. Their faces had turned blue. They no longer had the strength to cry out when waves washed over them. They just sat silently, waiting for death to come.

Benitez couldn't send these men back below deck. The 18 men down there were still struggling to save the submarine. The *Cochino*'s engines had stopped working. The men were trying to get them started again. As they worked, they battled explosion after explosion. Several of the sailors had been burned. One was so badly burned that he was near death.

There was only one thing Benitez could do. He would try to squeeze all the men from the main deck up onto the **bridge**. This small area at the very top of the submarine was meant to hold seven people. Somehow, Benitez managed to jam all the men onto it. Then Benitez took off his own shoes. He gave them to one of the barefoot men. He also gave up his jacket and sweater to two of the coldest men.

The nearest land was 200 miles away.

Onto the *Tusk*

Commander of the *Tusk*

Soon after that, the sailors below deck got the engines started again. By this time, the *Tusk* had reached the *Cochino*. For the next five hours, the *Tusk* slowly led the damaged *Cochino* toward land. But at 8:39 P.M., another explosion ripped through the *Cochino*. This one was worse than the earlier ones. It filled the engine room with fire and gas. There was nothing more anyone could do. The submarine began slowly sinking.

Benitez told the men below deck to join him on the bridge. They would all have to **abandon** ship. That meant getting on board the *Tusk*. In the rough waters of the Greenland Sea, that wouldn't be easy.

The *Tusk* pulled closer to the *Cochino*. High waves tossed the submarines back and forth like toys. Still, the men managed to place a thin **plank** between the two submarines. They walked across it one at a time. Somehow, they all made it. The last man to cross was Rafael Benitez. Just as he stepped onto the *Tusk*, the plank fell into the icy sea. Two minutes later, the U.S.S. *Cochino* slipped below the surface, never to be seen again.

Today, the U.S.S. *Cochino* lies deep within the Arctic waters.

Read and Remember — Finish the Sentence

❋ **Circle the best ending for each sentence.**

1. Rafael Benitez was in charge of the _____.
Greenland navy   U.S.S. *Tusk*   U.S.S. *Cochino*

2. In one of the battery rooms, _____.
gas exploded   a fight broke out   a computer failed

3. Benitez squeezed men onto the bridge to get them out of the _____.
Tusk's path   cold waves and rain   gas on the main deck

4. The crew finally made it _____.
onto the *Tusk*   to the Arctic Circle   below deck

5. In the end, the *Cochino* _____.
returned to the United States   sank   was towed to safety

Think About It — Drawing Conclusions

❋ **Write one or more sentences to answer each question.**

1. Why did Benitez order his crew to come up onto the main deck during the storm? _____

_____

2. Why did eighteen men stay below deck? _____

_____

3. Why were the men tied to the railing? _____

_____

4. Why did the *Tusk* have trouble reaching the *Cochino*? _____

_____

Focus on Vocabulary — Make a Word

Choose a word in dark print to complete each sentence. Write the letters of the word on the blanks. When you are finished, the letters in the circle will tell you one part of the *Cochino* that filled with fire and gas.

course	submarine	plank	abandon
lashed	overboard	gales	battery
bridge	explosion		

1. The men were in danger of being swept ____.

2. The crew of the *Cochino* finally had to ____ ship.

3. The *Cochino* was rocked by the storm's ____.

4. Benitez tried to squeeze all the men onto the ____.

5. The men had to cross a thin ____ to reach the *Tusk*.

6. An officer ____, or tied, the men to the railing.

7. The fire started in the ____ room.

8. The *Cochino* struggled to stay on ____.

9. The shaking was caused by a gas ____.

10. The *Cochino* was an underwater ship, or ____.

Countries

Some maps give information about countries. Thin lines are used to show the **borders** between countries. The map key explains what symbols are used on the map. This map shows the countries near the Arctic waters where the *Cochino* sank. Study the map and the map key. Write the answer to each question.

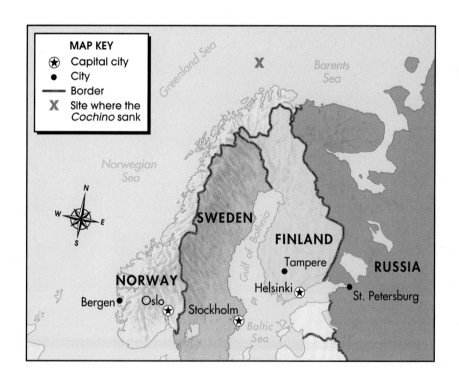

1. Which two countries share a border with Sweden? _____

_____

2. What is the capital city of Finland? _____

3. Of which country is Oslo the capital city? _____

4. Near the coast of which country did the *Cochino* sink? _____

5. In which country is St. Petersburg? _____

6. Which two countries have coasts on the Gulf of Bothnia? _____

_____

Footsteps to the South Pole

On November 3, 1985, Robert Swan, Roger Mear, and Gareth Wood left Hut Point, Antarctica. They began moving south on cross-country skis. If all went well, the three men would make it to the South Pole in 74 days. The group was following the path taken by explorer Robert Scott 74 years earlier. Scott and all his men died on this trail. Would the same thing happen to Swan, Mear, and Wood?

A Trip Just Like Scott's

Robert Swan had always been interested in Scott's story. In 1911 Scott and four others set out for the South Pole. They hoped to be the first ones there. Their journey was very difficult. When they reached the South Pole, they learned that Norway's Roald Amundsen had beaten them by 34 days. Disappointed, Scott and his men turned around. Then, during a bad blizzard, they ran out of food. All five men died. The bodies of Scott and two others were found just 11 miles from a **cache** of food and supplies.

Swan, Mear, and Wood decided to repeat Scott's trip to the South Pole. They wanted to know how it felt to walk nearly 900 miles through icy blizzards and roaring windstorms. Swan's group could have chosen to use modern safety equipment. For instance, they could have carried radios to call for help. They could have had helicopters fly food in to them. But they didn't. They wanted their trip to be just like Scott's. That way they would understand the courage, fear, and

loneliness he had felt. They called their expedition "In the Footsteps of Scott."

When Swan, Mear, and Wood left Hut Point, they each pulled 350-pound sledges. On these sledges were food, tents, and supplies. The sledges got lighter as the food was eaten. Still, it took great strength to pull each load over the rough, crusty ice.

The men traveled nine hours every day. They made their way through deep snow and bitterly cold winds. At the end of each day, they pitched tents and cooked supper. They were so exhausted that they could barely move. Still, the three men always tried to write a few notes about their day. They also took time to read Robert Scott's journal. That way, they could see how they were doing **compared** to him.

A Fall on the Ice

By November 24, the group had gone 215 miles across the barren **region**. That day, they hit a terrible blizzard. "Going rough, not able to see," wrote Swan.

Robert Scott died on his way back from the South Pole.

Swan and Mear pull their sledges across the ice.

"Each mile has to be fought for and won." Sixteen days later, they reached the foot of the Beardmore Glacier. At this point, they took off their skis. They put spikes on their boots. These spikes would help them keep from slipping on the glacier's icy surface.

By December 15, the men were part way up the huge glacier. Suddenly, Swan stepped into a crack in the ice. His foot stuck, causing him to fall. As he went down, he heard a **sickening** sound. The **ligaments** in his knee were tearing.

Right away, Swan knew he was in trouble. A sharp pain ripped through his leg. He wasn't sure he could stand. Then he looked around. Mear and Wood were way ahead of him. They hadn't seen him fall. They couldn't hear him, either. The harsh wind would drown out any cries for help.

"For perhaps the first time in my life I was truly frightened," Swan later said. He knew he had to get up and keep walking. If he didn't, he would die. "I forced myself to stand," he said. "Somehow... I managed to keep moving and caught up with my partners as they were making camp." By then, Swan's knee was badly **swollen**.

No Turning Back

Wood, meanwhile, had troubles of his own. He had a bad **blister** on his foot. It would not heal. So he was having trouble walking, too.

That night, the three men talked about what to do. They had come 471 miles. They had 424 miles still to go. They couldn't stop or even slow down. If they did, they would run out of food. Then all three might die. Swan and Wood would just have to do the best they could.

The group reached the top of the glacier and continued on. The **terrain** became easier, and they put their skis back on. By Christmas Day, the group had traveled 618 miles. Swan and Wood were feeling better. But all three men were terribly hungry. Their small portions of food didn't fill them up. They were losing weight and losing strength.

Finally, on January 11, 1986, Swan, Mear, and Wood saw a flag in the distance. It marked the South Pole. There, people were cheering. Swan, Mear, and Wood had done it. They had walked in the footsteps of Scott and **survived**.

At last, the three men reached the South Pole.

Read and Remember — Choose the Answer

❄ **Draw a circle around the correct answer.**

1. What happened to Robert Scott on his return trip from the South Pole?

   He met Roald Amundsen.   He got lost.   He died.

2. About how far did Swan's group have to go to reach the South Pole?

   250 miles   350 miles   900 miles

3. What did the group try to do at the end of each day?

   take photos   send radio messages   write about their day

4. What did the men use to climb Beardmore Glacier?

   spiked boots   skis   snowshoes

5. What part of his body did Swan hurt on the journey?

   his back   his knee   his shoulder

6. What did Swan's group see that meant they were near the South Pole?

   a cache of food   a flag   a ship

Write About It

❄ **Imagine you were a newspaper reporter in 1986. Write a short article, describing what Swan, Mear, and Wood did. Tell who, what, when, where, and why in your article.**

Focus on Vocabulary — Crossword Puzzle

Use the clues to complete the puzzle. Choose from the words in dark print.

loneliness	blister	cache	survived
ligaments	terrain	region	compared
sickening	swollen		

Across

2. sore bubble on the skin

6. sad feeling caused by being alone

8. place where food and supplies are hidden or stored

9. ground

10. stayed alive

Down

1. making one feel sick

3. parts of the body that connect bones

4. saw how two things were alike or different

5. area of land

7. increased in size

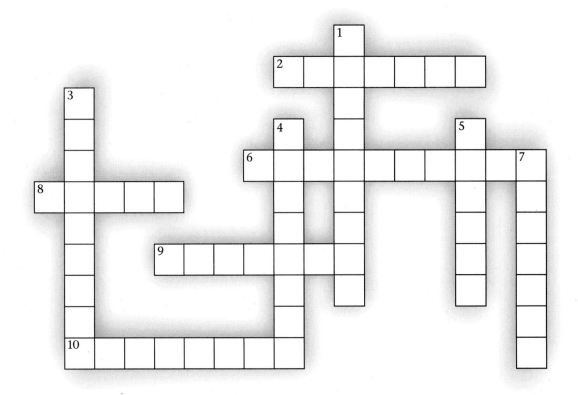

Map Keys

❋ Maps use different symbols or colors. A **map key** tells what the symbols or colors mean. This map shows the paths of four explorers who tried to reach the South Pole. Study the map and map key. Write the answer to each question below.

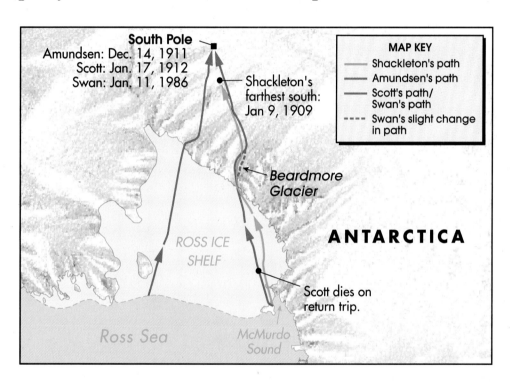

1. What color is Scott's path? _____

2. Which explorer did not reach the South Pole? _____

3. Which explorer started in a different area of the Ross Ice Shelf?

   _____

4. At what glacier did Swan change his path slightly from Scott's path?

   _____

5. What sea is near the explorers' starting points? _____

6. On what date did Amundsen reach the South Pole? _____

Among the Polar Bears

All her life, Helen Thayer enjoyed adventure. She had already climbed some of the world's highest mountains. She had won prizes in track and field contests. She had even been a United States champion **luge** racer. But she wanted more. So in 1988, at the age of 50, Thayer headed for Resolute Bay, Canada. There she began a 364-mile journey that no woman had ever made before. Many people thought she would never make it back alive.

Making Plans

Thayer's plan was to ski across ice all the way to the **North Magnetic Pole**. This pole is found among the islands of northern Canada. When a needle on a **compass** points north, it is pointing to this spot. The magnetic pole is hundreds of miles south of the Earth's most northern point, the North Pole. Still, it is a cold and lonely place. Blizzards, ice storms, and high winds can strike at any moment.

Thayer had planned to travel alone. But the Inuit of northern Canada told her to take along some dogs. She would need them, they said. Dogs would help scare off polar bears. Indeed, many polar bears lived along Thayer's planned **route**. These huge animals were known to **stalk** and kill humans.

At the last minute, Thayer agreed to take along one dog. She chose a four-year-old black dog named Charlie, who was part **husky**. It turned out to be a wise move. Thayer later said, "If I hadn't taken him with me, I might not be here today."

Thayer and Charlie set off across the ice.

On March 30, 1988, Thayer and Charlie set off. Thayer pulled a sledge that weighed 160 pounds. Charlie walked beside her. He was tied to a chain that hung from her waist.

A Brave Dog

The first day, Thayer got frostbite on her hands. By the next morning, the skin on her hands was blistered and sore. Thayer struggled to pack up her tent. As she did so, a polar bear moved silently over the white snow toward her. Luckily, Charlie spotted it. He started growling. That got Thayer's attention. She grabbed her **flare** gun. She shot it in the air, hoping to scare the bear away. After seven shots, the animal finally turned and moved off. Thayer saw two more polar bears before the day ended.

Three days later, another polar bear came after Thayer. This one could not be scared off so easily. Soon, it was just 20 feet away. Quickly, Thayer unhooked Charlie from his chain. "Charlie raced to the bear's leg and hung on," Thayer later said. "The bear tried to bite him, but Charlie twisted away." At last, said Thayer, "the bear broke away and ran off." Charlie had saved Thayer's life.

More Troubles

As Thayer continued, she met other polar bears. Each time she came across one, Charlie did his best to warn her. His growl told her when danger was near. Still, Thayer had some scary moments. One day she was stalked by a hungry polar bear for four frightening hours. Finally, the animal disappeared back into the frozen world of the Arctic.

Another day, a polar bear charged toward Thayer. It knocked aside the heavy sledge like it was "a tiny toothpick." Another attack frightened Thayer so badly that tears came to her eyes. In the freezing Arctic air, the tears quickly turned to ice. For a short while, Thayer's eyes were frozen shut!

On Day 20 of Thayer's journey, a windstorm kicked up without warning. The wind was so strong it knocked Thayer off her feet. It ripped her eye **goggles** off. Tiny bits of ice showered her face. They cut her skin and stung her eyes.

Thayer and Charlie stand proudly at the North Magnetic Pole.

When the storm finally ended, Thayer stared at her sledge. Most of her supplies had been blown away. Almost all her food was gone. The only thing left was a small bag of walnuts. Charlie had lost about half of his food.

Thayer still had a week's worth of skiing to go. To make the walnuts last that long, she allowed herself just five a day. Also, she now had only enough water to give herself a **pint** a day. Even so, Thayer didn't quit. Bravely she continued on across the **stark** white ice.

On Day 21, Thayer and Charlie reached the North Magnetic Pole. Tired and hungry, Thayer took many pictures and then headed on her way. She had a long way to go to get to the place where a plane would pick her up.

On Day 23, Thayer had to fight her way through thick fog. By then, she was weak from lack of food. She was also terribly thirsty. She tried eating ice. But that just made blood blisters in her mouth.

At last, Thayer and Charlie arrived at the pick-up point. Thayer radioed for a plane to pick them up. Her head hurt. She was dizzy. She was almost dead from lack of food and water. Still, she had met her goal. "I knew that I could do it," said Thayer happily.

Charlie had saved Thayer's life many times.

Read and Remember — Check the Events

❄ **Place a check in front of the three sentences that tell what happened in the story.**

_____ **1.** Thayer started her journey in Resolute Bay, Canada.

_____ **2.** Charlie ran away every time he saw a polar bear.

_____ **3.** Thayer found a baby polar bear and kept it as a pet.

_____ **4.** Thayer lost much of her food in a bad windstorm.

_____ **5.** A plane dropped extra food to Thayer during the last week.

_____ **6.** Once, Thayer's eyes became frozen shut.

Think About It— Find the Main Ideas

❄ **Underline the two most important ideas from the story.**

1. Helen Thayer became the first woman to travel to the North Magnetic Pole.

2. Charlie was a four-year-old black dog.

3. Thayer pulled a 160-pound sledge.

4. Thayer had several close calls on her Arctic journey.

5. Near the end of the trip, Thayer became dizzy.

6. Thayer got blood blisters in her mouth from eating ice.

Focus on Vocabulary — Match Up

❄ Match each word with its meaning. Write the correct letter on the blank.

_____ **1.** compass

_____ **2.** route

_____ **3.** North Magnetic Pole

_____ **4.** stalk

_____ **5.** goggles

_____ **6.** pint

_____ **7.** stark

_____ **8.** husky

_____ **9.** luge

_____ **10.** flare

a. sled used in speed races

b. special glasses worn to protect the eyes

c. kind of dog that can live in cold places

d. unit of measure for liquids

e. blaze of light

f. equipment used to show direction

g. path

h. gloomy and empty

i. follow someone quietly

j. northern spot to which a compass needle points

Latitude and Longitude

Lines that run east to west around Earth are lines of **latitude.** Lines that run north to south are lines of **longitude.** All the lines are measured in **degrees,** or **°.** Latitude and longitude can be used together to show a place's location. For example, Resolute Bay in Canada is at 75°N, 95°W. The latitude is written first, then the longitude. Study the map below. Circle the answer that best completes each sentence.

1. The latitude of the town of Clyde River is _____.

   71°S   68°E   71°N

2. One place that crosses the 80°W longitude is _____.

   Ellesmere Island   Beaufort Sea   Victoria Island

3. One island that crosses the 70°N latitude is _____.

   Victoria Island   Devon Island   Ellesmere Island

4. The town at 73°N, 77°W is _____.

   Pond Inlet   Qaanaaq   Cambridge Bay

Crossing Antarctica

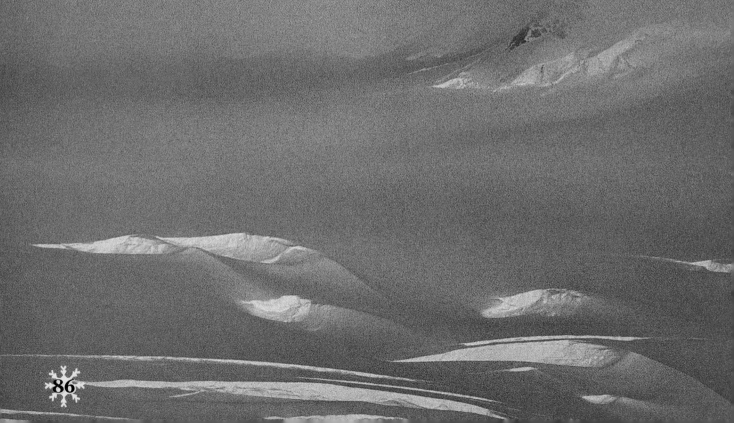

For thirty years, Will Steger dreamed of crossing Antarctica. Finally, he decided to do it. Steger, an American, put together a team of six men from six countries. The group planned to cross the continent using skis and dog sleds. They decided to take the longest and hardest route possible. They would go places no one had dared to travel. The men believed they could make it. But they knew that death could surprise them at any point along the way.

Difficult Travel

The six men set out from the tip of the Antarctic **Peninsula** on July 27, 1989. Ahead of them lay more than 3,700 miles of ice and snow. They took three sleds with them. These were filled with almost 3,000 pounds of food and supplies. Among the supplies were tools for gathering ice samples. The samples would help show **pollution** levels in Antarctica.

It took forty dogs to pull the sleds. The men skied alongside. Victor Boyarsky from Russia often led the way. Qin Dahe from China had never skied before. He had to learn as he went.

The traveling was hard right from the start of the trip. Deep crevasses in the ice blocked the way. The air was bitterly cold. High winds blew snow into the men's faces. At times, they couldn't even see their own hands. Keizo Finatsu from Japan said it was "like being inside a Ping-Pong ball."

Over the next few weeks, the weather got worse and worse. One storm lasted 60 days. Temperatures fell to

45 degrees below zero. The wind blew 100 miles an hour. The **wind-chill factor** made the temperature 110 degrees below zero.

Sticking Together

A crevasse

As the men fought through the wind and snow, they worked up big **appetites**. Their food supply **dwindled**. Steger and the others had planned for this. They had set up food caches along the way. Each one held enough food for two weeks. The caches were marked with nine-foot poles. That way the men would be sure to find them. But in Antarctica, even the best plans aren't always good enough. By the time the six men had gone 500 miles, they had missed two caches. Blowing snow had buried the nine-foot poles.

By then, all the men had frostbite on their cheeks. Their lips were cracked. The skin on their fingers had split open. The dogs were exhausted. It no longer looked as though the team could make it across Antarctica.

That's when Jean-Louis Etienne from France asked whether two or three of the men should be sent back.

The team was made up of six men from six different countries.

The dogs pulled the sleds, and the men skied alongside.

A smaller group might have a better chance. But no one liked that plan. Said Geoff Somers of England, "Either we all make it or none." By a vote of 6 to 0, the men agreed to push on together.

So on they plodded. They finally found some of their food caches. Also, a supply plane dropped some extra dog food down to them. Without that, the dogs would have starved to death.

On December 11, the group finally reached the South Pole. By then, they had traveled 2,071 miles. But they weren't done yet. Ahead of them lay the most **challenging** part of the continent. The team had to climb to an elevation of 11,400 feet. Waves of frozen ice made skiing almost impossible. After falling many times, Steger and Dahe chose to walk instead. One day, the men recorded their coldest temperature. It was 54 degrees below zero. Another day the wind-chill factor dropped to 125 degrees below zero.

Lost in a Blizzard

On February 28, 1990, the men were just 16 miles from the end of their journey. Suddenly, a killer storm moved in. The men pitched their tents and waited.

On March 1, at about 4:30 P.M., Keizo Funatsu from Japan went out to check on his dogs. He got lost in the swirling snow. By 6 P.M., the other men were worried. They went looking for Keizo. But they couldn't see anything through the wildly blowing snow. **Grimly**, they returned to their tents to wait for the end of the terrible storm.

Meanwhile, Keizo was trying to stay calm. He knew his friends would come looking for him when the storm ended. So he dug a **trench** in the snow and lay down. Soon the snow buried him completely. Later, he said, "My life seemed very small compared to nature, to Antarctica." Being inside the trench helped keep Keizo warm.

The next morning the storm still raged. Even so, the men **desperately** tried again to find Keizo. They held onto a long rope so they wouldn't get lost. Then they walked in a wide circle around their camp, calling Keizo's name. When he heard them, he jumped out of the snow. "I am alive! I am alive!" he shouted. The next day, the six men finished their **historic**, seven-month trip across Antarctica.

A blizzard moved in as the team neared the end of the journey.

Read and Remember — Finish the Sentence

❄ **Circle the best ending for each sentence.**

1. Steger and the other men set out across Antarctica on _____.
spiked boots   skis   snowshoes

2. The path chosen by the group was very _____.
flat   long   easy

3. The first two food caches were _____.
hidden by snow   stolen   destroyed by a blizzard

4. Jean-Louis Etienne suggested that two or three men _____.
bring a radio   search for the dogs   turn back

5. The journey across Antarctica took the men _____.
six weeks   seven months   two years

Write About It

❄ **Imagine you were Keizo Finatsu. Write a letter home, describing your night out in the blizzard.**

Dear _____,

_____

_____

_____

_____

_____

_____

USE WHAT YOU KNOW

Focus on Vocabulary — Find the Meaning

Read each sentence. Circle the best meaning for the word or words in dark print.

1. They set out from the Antarctic **Peninsula**.

   land mostly surrounded by water   lake   country

2. They planned to check **pollution** levels.

   air   harmful materials   sickness

3. The men were prepared for the **wind-chill factor**.

   how cold the air feels in wind   blowing snow   storm

4. The six men had big **appetites**.

   ideas of teamwork   tents   feelings of hunger

5. The food supply **dwindled**.

   kept them alive   became smaller   was hard to find

6. Ahead lay the most **challenging** part of the journey.

   pleasant   difficult   famous

7. **Grimly**, Steger's group returned to their tents.

   with a feeling of gloom   one by one   scared

8. Keizo Finatsu dug a **trench** during a storm.

   narrow ditch   pocket of air   place for supplies

9. The men tried **desperately** to find Keizo.

   in total darkness   with loud noises   with little hope

10. The men finally finished their **historic** trip.

    very tiring   important in history   exciting

Distance Scale

Will Steger traveled more than 3,700 miles across Antarctica. On a map, use a **distance scale** to find the distance between two places. On this map of Antarctica, the distance scale shows that 1 inch stands for 800 miles of land. Use a ruler to measure the distances on the map. Circle the correct answer to each question.

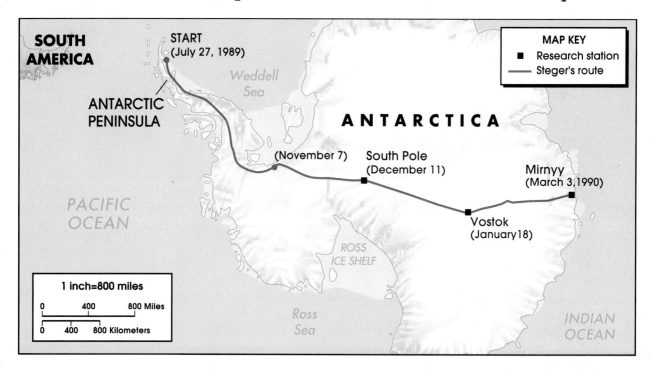

1. About how many inches are between the November 7 point and the South Pole on the map?

   1 inch   2 inches   3 inches

2. What is the actual distance between the November 7 point and the South Pole?

   400 miles   800 miles   1,600 miles

3. How far did Steger travel from December 11 to March 3?

   3,700 miles   950 miles   1,900 miles

4. Which place is about 350 miles from the South Pole?

   Weddell Sea   Mirnyy   Ross Ice Shelf

A Long Wait

Nikita Ovsyannikov came from Russia. Rory McGuinness was born in Australia. Tatsuhiko Kobayashi was Japanese. Even though these men came from different parts of the world, they all shared one goal. They wanted to make a movie about polar bears. On September 2, 1998, they headed to Wrangel Island, near the northeast coast of Russia. But the men soon found out that getting off the island was a lot harder than getting on.

Trapped!

Wrangel Island is a barren, ice-covered place. About twenty people live in a village there. But the **filmmakers** didn't want to be near people. So they headed to a small hut eighty miles from the village. That way, the three men were free to watch the polar bears in their natural **habitat**.

The work went well. The men filmed the polar bears swimming. They filmed them playing, eating, and just resting on the ice-covered **tundra**. They also filmed walruses that visited the island. But the men had to work quickly. During the fall, there are only a few hours of daylight in the Arctic region. Each day, the three filmmakers felt the air growing colder. Each day, the darkness came more quickly. By the middle of October, the men had just three hours of sunlight a day.

On October 15, the men were ready to go home. A helicopter was supposed to pick them up. But that day a terrible blizzard roared across Wrangel Island. No

The men filmed polar bears in their natural habitat.

helicopter could make it through the fierce wind and blowing snow.

The following day, it snowed again. Once more, the men were stuck on the island. Days later, it was still snowing. Weather in the far north is often cold and stormy. But this was worse than anyone expected. It just would not stop snowing.

Sitting in the Darkness

After a week or two, the men began to feel trapped. They had a **mobile** phone. They also had computers with **e-mail**. So they could send messages back and forth with people in other parts of the world. But they had to be careful. They didn't want to run down the batteries.

As the days dragged by, blizzards continued to hit the island. Temperatures dropped to 22 degrees below zero. High winds whistled past the little hut where the filmmakers **huddled**. At night, polar bears clawed at the door. "It was practically complete darkness and snowstorms," said Kobayashi. "We had nothing to do but stay in our hut."

Each man had brought one book in his own language. So they spent some time reading. But they grew tired of reading the same book over and over again. Besides, they didn't want to use up all their fuel by running the lamp. "So we sat in the darkness," said Kobayashi. "We were sitting there listening to the sound of the snowstorms outside. It drove me to **despair**."

Running Out of Food

The men tried to divide their food carefully. Many times they made a meal out of nothing but cold **porridge** and rice. All three men began to lose weight. By the end of six weeks, they were running out of food. Their meat was gone. All they had left was some grain, beans, sugar, and tea. Even that would have been gone in another two or three days. If the weather did not clear soon, the men would starve to death. "They are very weak," said John Hyde, another filmmaker who spoke to the men on the phone. "It's pretty serious."

The village on the island was eighty miles away.

Rescue helicopter

The villagers on the other side of Wrangel Island tried to help. They packed up **snowmobiles** with food and tried to reach the men. But bad weather forced them to turn back. There was just too much wind and snow to travel across the island.

Other rescuers considered trying to reach the men by sea. But the icy waters made it too hard for ships to get to the island.

At last, on December 1, there was a break in the storms. The sky cleared up enough for rescuers to try again. No one knew how long the good weather would last. So a helicopter rushed to Wrangel Island. The three men threw their film and supplies onto the helicopter. Then the pilot hurried them back through the darkness to the Russian **mainland**.

Ovsyannikov, McGuinness, and Kobayashi were thin and weak. But they were happy to be safe. They also were thankful to be going home. It was scary to think what might have happened to them. Said Kobayashi, "I'm happy that we're not buried in that hut under the snow."

The three men were glad to be rescued from the island at last.

Read and Remember — Choose the Answer

Draw a circle around the correct answer.

1. Why did the three men go to Wrangel Island?

to avoid people   to make a movie   to study Arctic plants

2. What kept the men from getting off the island?

broken ship   blizzards   darkness

3. What clawed at the door of the men's hut?

wolves   foxes   polar bears

4. Who tried to travel across Wrangel Island to reach the men?

villagers   scientists   students

5. What did the men almost run out of?

medicine   food   paper

6. What was used to rescue the men?

snowmobiles   a ship   a helicopter

Think About It — Fact or Opinion

A fact is a true statement. An opinion is a statement that tells what a person thinks. Write F beside each statement that is a fact. Write O beside each statement that is an opinion.

_____ **1.** Walruses sometimes visited Wrangel Island.

_____ **2.** The hardest part was the long hours of total darkness.

_____ **3.** As time passed, the three men began to lose weight.

_____ **4.** The men never should have gone to Wrangel Island.

_____ **5.** It is exciting to watch polar bears playing.

_____ **6.** The men avoided using the lamp to save fuel.

USE WHAT YOU KNOW

Focus on Vocabulary — Finish the Paragraphs

Use the words in dark print to complete the paragraphs. Reread the paragraphs to be sure they make sense.

habitat	**porridge**	**filmmakers**	**e-mail**
mobile	**huddled**	**snowmobiles**	**despair**
tundra	**mainland**		

In the fall of 1998, three (1)_____ went to Wrangel Island near Russia. They filmed polar bears in their natural (2)_____. By mid-October, they were ready to leave. But terrible snowstorms started to blow across the ice-covered (3)_____. The men were trapped on the island. Luckily, they had a (4)_____ phone with them. They also used computers to send messages by (5)_____.

For six long weeks, the men (6)_____ in their small hut. People tried to reach them on (7)_____ and in helicopters. But the snowstorms were too fierce. Kobayashi said the sound of the storms drove him to (8)_____.

Soon, the three men began to run out of food. At some meals, they only ate cold (9)_____ and rice. Then on December 1, the sky began to clear. At last, the men were brought safely back to the Russian (10)_____.

100

Countries

Some maps give information about countries. Thin lines are used to show the **borders** between countries. The map key explains what symbols are used on the map. This map shows eastern Russia and nearby countries. Study the map and the map key. Write the answer to each question.

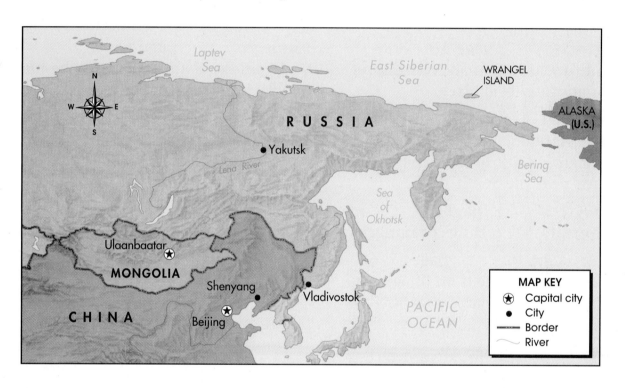

1. Which two countries share Mongolia's borders? _____

2. In which country is the city Yakutsk? _____

3. What is the capital city of China? _____

4. What Russian river is shown on the map? _____

5. Which country has a coast along the Sea of Okhotsk? _____

6. In which country is the city Shenyang? _____

GLOSSARY

Ⓢ Words with this symbol can be found in the USE A MAP activities.

abandon   page 66
To abandon means to go away from or to leave.

airship   page 55
An airship is a large flying machine. It is lighter than air.

altitude   page 16
Altitude is height above sea level or another level place.

Antarctic Circle   pages 45, 47
Ⓢ The Antarctic Circle is an imaginary line around the area near the South Pole.

appetites   page 88
Appetites are feelings of hunger.

Arctic Circle   pages 7, 61
Ⓢ The Arctic Circle is an imaginary line around the area near the North Pole.

barren   page 49
Barren means not able to grow anything.

battery   page 63
A battery is equipment used to make electricity.

bay   page 7
A bay is an area of water that is partly surrounded by land.

bitterly   page 7
Bitterly means painfully.

blister   page 74
A blister is a sore bubble on the skin.

blizzard   page 24
A blizzard is a heavy snowstorm with strong winds.

borders   pages 69, 101
Ⓢ Borders are the lines that separate countries or other areas.

bridge   page 65
A bridge is an area above the main deck of a ship from which the ship is controlled.

buoys   page 16
Buoys are objects that float. They are usually used as markers in water.

cache   page 71
A cache is a place where food and supplies are hidden or stored.

cape   page 39
A cape is a point of land that sticks out into the sea.

carrier pigeons   page 16
Carrier pigeons are birds trained to carry messages.

challenging   page 89
Challenging means difficult.

cliffs   page 55
Cliffs are high, steep walls of ice or rock.

collapsed   page 42
Collapsed means fell down.

commander   page 31
A commander is a leader.

companions   page 24
Companions are friends or people who go places together.

compared   page 72
Compared means saw how two things are alike or different.

compass   page 79
A compass is equipment used to show direction, such as north or south.

compass rose   page 29
🌐 A compass rose is a symbol on a map that shows direction.

continent   pages 13, 47
🌐 A continent is a very large body of land, such as Antarctica.

course   page 63
A course is a path or route.

crevasses   page 40
Crevasses are deep cracks in rock or in ice.

cruise   page 55
A cruise is a slow trip on a boat or ship for fun.

current   page 8
A current is water flowing in a certain direction.

degrees   pages 9, 37, 85
🌐 Degrees are units of measure for temperature or distance.

despair   page 97
Despair is a total lack of hope or a sense of defeat.

desperately   page 90
Desperately means almost without hope.

disappearance   page 56
A disappearance is the act of going out of sight.

dismal   page 47
Dismal means causing gloom.

distance scale   page 93
🌐 A distance scale compares distance on a map with distance in the real world.

dwindled   page 88
Dwindled means became smaller.

eerie   page 57
Eerie means strange and spooky.

elevation   page 41
Elevation is height above a given level, such as sea level.

e-mail   page 96
E-mail, or electronic mail, is a way computer users send messages to one another.

equator   page 53
🌐 The equator is an imaginary circle that runs east and west around Earth. It divides Earth equally into north and south.

exhausted   page 17
Exhausted means very tired or worn out.

expedition   page 15
An expedition is a long journey taken for a reason, such as to explore an area.

explosion   page 63
An explosion is the act of blowing up or breaking up with great force and noise.

failure   page 42
A failure is the act of not completing a goal or task.

fierce   page 25
Fierce means dangerous and strong.

filmmakers   page 95
Filmmakers are people who make movies.

flare   page 80
A flare is a blaze of light that is used to signal someone or to light up an area.

floe   page 9
A floe is a huge chunk of ice floating in the ocean.

formations   page 58
Formations are things that have been shaped.

former   page 31
Former means in the past.

frostbite   page 26
Frostbite is the freezing of a part of the body, such as a toe.

gales   page 63
Gales are very strong winds.

glacier   page 41
A glacier is a large sheet of ice and snow that moves very slowly.

glorious   page 16
Glorious means wonderful or grand.

goggles   page 81
Goggles are special glasses worn to protect the eyes.

grimly   page 90
Grimly means with a feeling of gloom.

habitat   page 95
A habitat is a place where an animal or a plant usually lives.

harsh   page 58
Harsh means rough and not pleasant.

hemispheres   page 53
If the world is divided in half, it is divided into two hemispheres.

hesitate   page 56
To hesitate means to stop and wait before acting.

historic   page 90
Historic means important or famous in history.

hostile   page 55
Hostile means very unfriendly.

huddled   page 96
Huddled means crowded together.

husky   page 79
A husky is a kind of dog that has a heavy coat and can live in cold places.

iceberg   page 48
An iceberg is a huge block of floating ice.

ice shelf   page 50
An ice shelf is a huge wall of ice.

igloos   page 9
Igloos are small houses made of snow or ice.

inland page 25
Inland means an area of land away from the coast.

jagged page 34
Jagged means sharp and rough.

kayaks page 9
Kayaks are canoes with covered frames.

lashed page 65
Lashed means tied with a rope.

latitude pages 34, 37, 85
Lines of latitude are imaginary lines that run east and west around Earth. They measure distance in degrees north and south of the equator.

lead page 32
A lead is an area of open water.

ligaments page 73
Ligaments are parts of the body that hold bones together.

loneliness page 72
Loneliness is a sad feeling caused by being alone.

longitude pages 37, 85
Lines of longitude are imaginary lines that run north and south around Earth. They measure distance in degrees east and west of the 0° longitude.

luge page 79
A luge is a racing sled.

mainland page 98
Mainland means the main part of a country or a continent.

map key pages 21, 77
A map key tells what the symbols, colors, or patterns on a map mean.

mobile page 96
Mobile means able to be moved from place to place.

mountain range page 24
A mountain range is a group of similar mountains that are close together.

native page 7
Native means originally from a certain place or country.

navigate page 58
To navigate means to steer or guide a ship.

northernmost page 31
Northernmost means the farthest north.

North Magnetic Pole page 79
The North Magnetic Pole is the spot in the Arctic to which a compass needle points.

North Pole page 7
The North Pole is the point on Earth that is the farthest north.

overboard page 64
Overboard means over the side of a ship into the water.

pack ice page 18
Pack ice is large blocks of ice that are jammed together.

peninsula page 87
A peninsula is a long area of land that is almost totally surrounded by water.

pickaxes   page 33
Pickaxes are sharp, heavy tools that are used to break up rocks, soil, or ice.

pint   page 82
A pint is a unit of measure for liquids. A pint equals 16 fluid ounces, or 2 cups.

plagued   page 33
Plagued means troubled or bothered.

plank   page 66
A plank is a thick, heavy board.

plunged   page 24
Plunged means fell suddenly.

pollution   page 87
Pollution is the act of putting harmful materials in air, soil, or water.

porridge   page 97
Porridge is a soft cereal or soup made by boiling oatmeal or another food in water or milk.

portions   page 41
Portions are helpings of food.

pressure ridges   page 32
Pressure ridges are places where huge ice floes have been pushed on top of each other.

region   page 72
A region is an area of land.

rescuers   page 23
Rescuers are people who help others who are hurt or are in dangerous places.

route   page 79
A route is a path or a road.

scientific   page 50
Scientific means having to do with science.

shoreline   page 25
A shoreline is the line where land meets a body of water.

sickening   page 73
Sickening means making one feel sick.

sledges   page 15
Sledges are sleds used to carry loads across ice.

snow blindness   page 39
Snow blindness is the condition of not being able to see because of bright sunlight reflecting off snow.

snowmobiles   page 98
Snowmobiles are sled-like machines with motors. They are made to travel over snow.

sound   page 48
A sound is a long, wide stretch of water that connects larger bodies of water.

South Pole   page 39
The South Pole is the point on Earth that is the farthest south.

stalk   page 79
To stalk means to follow someone quietly.

stark   page 82
Stark means gloomy and empty.

stranded   page 23
People are stranded if they are not able to get out of a place.

submarine   page 63
A submarine is a ship that travels underwater.

suffered   page 39
Suffered means put up with or felt pain.

survived   page 74
Survived means stayed alive.

swollen   page 73
Swollen means increased in size.

terrain   page 74
Terrain is the surface of the land. It is easy to travel on smooth terrain.

tragedy   page 18
A tragedy is a very unhappy or terrible event.

trench   page 90
A trench is a narrow ditch dug into land or snow.

tundra   page 95
Tundra is a treeless area of flat land in the Arctic. The ground below the tundra is always frozen.

unknown   page 15
The unknown is something that people do not know about.

valuable   page 32
Valuable means very important.

vessel   page 48
A vessel is a ship or large boat.

wind-chill factor   page 88
Wind-chill factor is what the temperature feels like when the wind is blowing. It feels cooler outside when the wind is blowing.

zigzag   page 50
Zigzag means moving back and forth in a series of sharp turns.

Did You Know?

◄ How long is a day in the polar regions? At the North Pole and at the South Pole, there are six months of darkness and six months of light. That means the sun rises and sets only once a year at the poles!

Do you know what bird ▶ migrates, or moves, farther than any other bird in the world? In one year, the small Arctic tern flies from the Arctic areas of Canada or Siberia to the South Pole and back again. That's more than 20,000 miles each year!

◄ What is the longest animal in the world? Some people might answer the blue whale, which is the largest animal. But the longest animal is the Arctic lion's mane. This Arctic jellyfish can reach up to 200 feet in length. That's about the length of 2 blue whales, or 20 elephants!

◀ Is there really a pole at the South Pole? Yes, there is. It's a barber's pole topped by a mirrored ball. It was put there by people working at the research station at the South Pole.

Where do plants and animals ▶ live in Antarctica? They can only live near the coasts. Temperatures at the coasts are much milder than in other places in Antarctica. In winter it can be as cold as –13°F at the coast, but it can be as cold as –115°F inland.

◀ What is one difference between Antarctica and the Arctic region? Antarctica is ice with land below it. In some places the ice is more than two miles thick. Much of the Arctic region is ice floating over water. But this ice is usually only about six feet thick!

CHART YOUR SCORES

Score Your Work

1. Count the number of correct answers you have for each activity.
2. Write these numbers in the boxes in the chart.
3. Give yourself a score (maximum of 5 points) for **Write About It**.
4. Add up the numbers to get a final score for each tale.
5. Write your final score in the score box.
6. Compare your final score with the maximum score given for each story.

Tales	Read and Remember	Think About It	Write About It	Focus on Vocabulary	Use a Map	Score
Trapped by the Ice						/24
Arctic Flight						/25
The 3,000-Mile Walk						/25
To the North Pole!						/19
Almost There						/24
Japan Enters the Race						/27
In Search of Her Hero						/22
Trouble in Arctic Waters						/25
Footsteps to the South Pole						/27
Among the Polar Bears						/19
Crossing Antarctica						/24
A Long Wait						/28

ANSWER KEY

Trapped by the Ice

Pages 6–13
Read and Remember — Check the Events:
Sentences 1, 2, 5
Write About It: Answers will vary.
Focus on Vocabulary — Crossword Puzzle:
ACROSS — 5. igloos 6. Arctic Circle 7. degrees
9. bay 10. native; DOWN — 1. bitterly 2. floe
3. North Pole 4. current 8. kayaks
Use a Map — Continents and Oceans:
1. North America, South America, Africa, Australia,
Asia, Europe, Antarctica 2. Europe, Asia, North
America 3. Indian Ocean, Pacific Ocean
4. Atlantic Ocean 5. Indian Ocean 6. Antarctica

Arctic Flight

Pages 14–21
Read and Remember — Finish the Sentence:
1. two months 2. a boat 3. ice weighing it
down 4. White Island 5. found 33 years later
Think About It — Cause and Effect:
1. c 2. d 3. a 4. b
Focus on Vocabulary — Finish Up:
1. sledges 2. exhausted 3. expedition 4. tragedy
5. glorious 6. carrier pigeons 7. pack ice
8. unknown 9. buoys 10. altitude
Use a Map — Map Keys:
1. ⊕ 2. Longyearbyen 3. no 4. Danes Island
5. no 6. White Island

The 3,000-Mile Walk

Pages 22–29
Read and Remember — Choose the Answer:
1. ice 2. Sea Horse Island 3. by walking 4. to
find the beach 5. in a snow cave 6. a house
Write About It: Answers will vary.
Focus on Vocabulary — Make a Word:
1. rescuers 2. companions 3. shoreline 4. blizzard
5. fierce 6. frostbite 7. stranded 8. plunged
9. mountain range 10. inland
The letters in the circles should spell *California*.
Use a Map — Map Directions:
1. north 2. east 3. northwest 4. southwest

To the North Pole!

Pages 30–37
Read and Remember — Check the Events:
Sentences 1, 3, 4
Think About It — Find the Main Ideas:
Sentences 1, 5
Focus on Vocabulary — Find the Meaning:
1. leader 2. in the past 3. farthest north 4. area
of open water 5. important 6. stacked ice floes
7. sharp tools 8. troubled 9. sharp and rough
10. distance from the equator
Use a Map — Latitude and Longitude:
1. 36°N 2. 122°W 3. Cairo 4. Sydney

Almost There

Pages 38–45
Read and Remember — Finish the Sentence:
1. foot 2. hidden crevasses 3. frostbite 4. pony
food 5. 360 miles
Write About It: Answers will vary.
Focus on Vocabulary — Finish the Paragraphs:
1. Cape 2. South Pole 3. suffered 4. snow
blindness 5. portions 6. crevasses 7. Glacier
8. elevation 9. failure 10. collapsed
Use a Map — Antarctic Circle:
1. South America 2. South Pole 3. Ross Ice Shelf
4. 90°S

Japan Enters the Race

Pages 46–53
Read and Remember — Choose the Answer:
1. a few students 2. an old sailing boat
3. icebergs 4. Roald Amundsen 5. climbed
the Ross Ice Shelf 6. as a hero
Think About It — Find the Sequence:
5, 1, 4, 2, 6, 3
Focus on Vocabulary — Match Up:
1. f 2. c 3. h 4. i 5. j 6. a 7. d 8. b 9. e 10. g
Use a Map — Hemispheres:
1. Northern Hemisphere 2. Eastern Hemisphere
3. Northern Hemisphere 4. Eastern and Southern
Hemispheres 5. Eastern, Western, and Southern
Hemispheres

In Search of Her Hero

Pages 54–61

Read and Remember — Check the Events:
Sentences 1, 3, 6

Write About It: Answers will vary.

Focus on Vocabulary — Finish Up:
1. airship 2. cruise 3. navigate 4. hesitate
5. hostile 6. cliffs 7. eerie 8. harsh
9. disappearance 10. formations

Use a Map — Arctic Circle:
1. Russia 2. North Pole 3. Norwegian Sea 4. 90°N

Trouble in Arctic Waters

Pages 62–69

Read and Remember — Finish the Sentence:
1. U.S.S. *Cochino* 2. gas exploded 3. cold waves
and rain 4. onto the *Tusk* 5. sank

Think About It — Drawing Conclusions:
1. He didn't want the men to breathe the
dangerous gas below deck. 2. They tried to bring
the fire under control. 3. They were tied to the
railing so that they wouldn't be washed overboard
by a strong wave. 4. The storm kept the *Tusk*
bobbing and rolling in the water. Also, the *Tusk's*
crewmen had to rescue men in the water.

Focus on Vocabulary — Make a Word:
1. overboard 2. abandon 3. gales 4. bridge
5. plank 6. lashed 7. battery 8. course
9. explosion 10. submarine
The letters in the circles should spell *engine room*.

Use a Map — Countries:
1. Norway, Finland 2. Helsinki 3. Norway
4. Norway 5. Russia 6. Sweden, Finland

Footsteps to the South Pole

Pages 70–77

Read and Remember — Choose the Answer:
1. He died. 2. 900 miles 3. write about their day
4. spiked boots 5. his knee 6. a flag

Write About It: Answers will vary.

Focus on Vocabulary — Crossword Puzzle:
ACROSS — 2. blister 6. loneliness 8. cache
9. terrain 10. survived; DOWN — 1. sickening
3. ligaments 4. compared 5. region 7. swollen

Use a Map — Map Keys:
1. red 2. Shackleton 3. Amundsen 4. Beardmore
Glacier 5. Ross Sea 6. December 14, 1911

Among the Polar Bears

Pages 78–85

Read and Remember — Check the Events:
Sentences 1, 4, 6

Think About It — Find the Main Ideas:
Sentences 1, 4

Focus on Vocabulary — Match Up:
1. f 2. g 3. j 4. i 5. b 6. d 7. h 8. c 9. a 10. e

Use a Map — Latitude and Longitude:
1. 71°N 2. Ellesmere Island 3. Victoria Island
4. Pond Inlet

Crossing Antarctica

Pages 86–93

Read and Remember — Finish the Sentence:
1. skis 2. long 3. hidden by snow 4. turn back
5. seven months

Write About It: Answers will vary.

Focus on Vocabulary — Find the Meaning:
1. land mostly surrounded by water 2. harmful
materials 3. how cold the air feels in wind
4. feelings of hunger 5. became smaller
6. difficult 7. with a feeling of gloom 8. narrow
ditch 9. with little hope 10. important in history

Use a Map — Distance Scale:
1. 1 inch 2. 800 miles 3. 1,900 miles 4. Ross
Ice Shelf

A Long Wait

Pages 94–101

Read and Remember — Choose the Answer:
1. to make a movie 2. blizzards 3. polar
bears 4. villagers 5. food 6. a helicopter

Think About It — Fact or Opinion:
1. F 2. O 3. F 4. O 5. O 6. F

Focus on Vocabulary — Finish the Paragraphs:
1. filmmakers 2. habitat 3. tundra 4. mobile
5. e-mail 6. huddled 7. snowmobiles 8. despair
9. porridge 10. mainland

Use a Map — Countries:
1. Russia, China 2. Russia 3. Beijing 4. Lena
River 5. Russia 6. China